HIKING GRAND TETON
& JACKSON HOLE TRAILS

Hiking Grand Teton & Jackson Hole Trails

by Carl Schreier

HOMESTEAD PUBLISHING
MOOSE, WYOMING

For Bill and Diane Tjenos.
Great friends, great food, great times.

Photography, unless noted on page 215, botanical and some other illustrations by the author, Carl Schreier.

ISBN 0-943972-21-3

Library of Congress Cataloging-in Publication Data
Schreier, Carl.
     Hiking Grand Teton and Jackson Hole Trails / by Carl Schreier.
— 1st ed.
          p.   cm.
     Includes bibliographical references (p.   ) and index.
     ISBN 0-943972-21-3 (paperback : alk. paper)
     1. Hiking—Wyoming—Grand Teton National Park—Guide-
books. 2. Hiking—Wyoming—Jackson Hole—Guidebooks. 3. Trails—
Wyoming—Grand Teton National Park—Guidebooks. 4. Trails—
Wyoming—Jackson Hole—Guidebooks. 5. Grand Teton National Park
(Wyo.)—Guidebooks. 6. Jackson Hole (Wyo.)—Guidebooks.   I. Title.
GV199.42.G662S35 1998
796.51'09787'55—dc21   98-23660
                                          CIP

First Edition
Printed in the United States of America on recycled, acid free paper.

1   3   5   7   9   10   8   6   4   2

Published by
HOMESTEAD PUBLISHING
Box 193 • Moose, Wyoming 83012

CONTENTS

Hiking Grand Teton
& Jackson Hole Trails

Hiking Grand Teton & Jackson Hole Trails

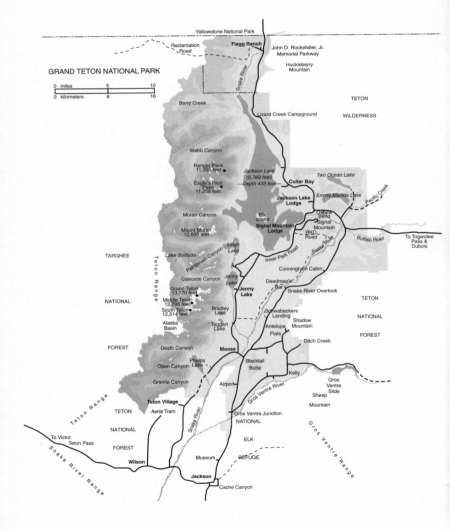

Yellowstone National Park

Reclamation Road

Flagg Ranch

John D. Rockefeller, Jr.
Memorial Parkway

Huckleberry Mountain

GRAND TETON NATIONAL PARK

| 0 | miles | 5 | 10 |
| 0 | kilometers | 8 | 16 |

Berry Creek

Lizard Creek Campground

TETON

WILDERNESS

Webb Canyon

Ranger Peak
11,355 feet

*Jackson Lake
(6,769 feet)
Depth 433 feet*

Two Ocean Lake

Colter Bay

Eagle's Rest
Peak
11,258 feet

Emma Matilda Lake

Pacific Creek

Moran Canyon

Elk
Island

**Jackson Lake
Lodge**

Oxbow
Bend

Signal
Mountain

**Signal Mountain
Lodge**

Mount Moran
12,605 feet

*Leigh
Lake*

RKO
Road

Snake River

Buffalo River

To Togwotee
Pass &
Dubois

TARGHEE

T
e
t
o
n

R
a
n
g
e

Lake Solitude

Lake

Paintbrush Canyon

Inner Park Road

Cunningham Cabin

Cascade Canyon

Jenny
Lake

Deadman's
Bar

NATIONAL

Grand Teton
13,770 feet

**Jenny
Lake**

Snake River Overlook

TETON

Middle Teton
12,798 feet

Bradley
Lake

South Teton
12,514 feet

Schwabackers
Landing

NATIONAL

Alaska
Basin

Taggart
Lake

Shadow
Mountain

Antelope
Flats

FOREST

FOREST

Death Canyon

Moose

Ditch Creek

Phelps
Lake

Blacktail
Butte

Open Canyon

Kelly

Gros
Ventre
Slide

Granite Canyon

Airport

Gros Ventre River

Sheep
Mountain

T
e
t
o
n

R
a
n
g
e

Teton Village

Aerial Tram

*Snake
River*

Gros Ventre Junction

NATIONAL

G
r
o
s

V
e
n
t
r
e

R
a
n
g
e

TETON

NATIONAL

ELK

To Victor
Teton Pass

FOREST

Museum

REFUGE

Snake River Range

Wilson

Jackson

Cache Canyon

INTRODUCTION

ABOUT THOSE TRAILS

Only a few locations on earth have the extensive trail system that exist in this region. Nearly 1,500 miles of trails wander the valleys and mountains of Jackson Hole. Yellowstone's trail system adds another 1,200 miles and the surrounding forests with possibly another 1,500 miles. In all nearly 4,000 miles of interconnected trails exist for the hiking spirit.

Originally many of these trails developed from game paths, used by migrating deer, elk, bear and antelope that moved between summer and winter foraging. These existing paths in turn were utilized by the first explorers and trappers who ventured into the region.

THE GRAND TETON, CENTER OF HIKING.

By the turn of the nineteenth century dude ranching and horse packing extended and connected the trail system and by the 1930s the Civil Conservation Corps (CCC) played the last vital role in improving trails into the system that exists today. With minor exceptions these trails have changed very little since then.

This hiking guide introduces this vast network of trails and is an invitation to the byways of Grand Teton National Park and Jackson Hole, Wyoming.

A KEY TO EXTRA TRAIL ACTIVITIES.

 Skiing   Canoeing   Bicycling    Dogs   Horses

---

WEATHER FORECASTING—PREDICTING THE UNPREDICTABLE

Jackson Hole and Grand Teton are well-known for their extremes in temperature, atmospheric pressure, seasons, terrain, latitude and elevation. Any one of these, or a combination, can trigger sudden and severe weather conditions. When on a mountain trail it is imperative to ones survival to always be prepared for any extreme weather condition. Even on bright, sunny, summer days, carry a lightweight jacket that also serves as rain protection. On warm, sunny winter days, carry gear appropriate for spending the night out, because it may be necessary.

Print, broadcast and televised weather forecasts are available for Jackson, but do not rely on them. Because the nearest NOAA (National Oceanic Atmospheric Administration) office—also known as the National Weather Service—whose responsibility it is to monitor and predict weather patterns, is located in Pocatello, Idaho. Their nearest field stations are located in Butte, Montana, and Lander, Wyoming. This leaves Yellowstone and Jackson Hole essentially in a black hole for weather monitoring. Coupled with this the mountains create their own weather, and it is forever and rapidly changing. Over some areas where there is an unobstructed view—such as Jackson Lake—it is possible to witness a rainstorm, snowstorm, sunshine, hail, lightning and a rainbow all at the same time.

Each year also brings its own set of patterns, so weather conditions of one year do not necessarily indicate the same conditions in any other given year. This basic Jackson Hole weather rule often is ignored. This misguidance has probably been the leading cause of exposure, or even death.

On a local and limited scale, however, most of Jackson Hole's storms advance from the southwest. By watching that horizon, it is possible to predict short-term weather conditions. Another helpful way to predict weather change is to know cloud formations. Special weather and atmospheric field guides are available to help identify cloud and sky formations and their associated weather conditions.

But once you are prepared for the worst conditions some seasons, especially summers can be wonderful, warm and dry for hiking. April through June often is wet, with occasional snow flurries into June. In fact, many trails will be snow-covered through this time. Spring and summer begin later here in the mountains than lower elevations, usually by two to four weeks later. By July and August the days and nights are warm and are the two major months for hiking. They

also represent the active time for mosquitoes and flies. Near the end of August, a perceptible decrease in daylight can be sensed, as well as the turning of the season. By September, frosty nights once again are common, but the days usually are warm and sunny. By mid-September, though, prevailing conditions can vary from warm and sunny to blustery and snowy. This weather can continue into October, with conditions and daylight declining progressively. Winter usually sets in by late October or early November and locks in until mid March or mid April, when spring begins to surface again.

Fall is a popular time for many hikers. The days can be warm and sunny and, best of all, there are fewer biting insects. On the down side, though, the forest trails are quiet because they lack chatter of migrant birds. Know the weather, use your own best judgement and prepare accordingly.

BY STUDYING CLOUD FORMATIONS IT IS POSSIBLE TO FORECAST WEATHER CONDITIONS.

NAVIGATING—READING MAP AND COMPASS

One of the most important hiking essentials is a good, accurate map. A companion map to this hiking guide is available. It is current and represents trails described in this book, offering a complete view of the valley and surrounding environs. Other maps are available as well. The United States Geological Survey (USGS) has published a series of maps; the general park map and its series of 7 ½-minute maps (referring to minutes of latitude and longitude) are adequate, but dated. Most USGS maps were surveyed and completed during the 1950s. Since then, most of the road locations have changed, and many trails either have been abandoned, relocated or were listed in error.

The surrounding forests also have published maps to their management lands. These maps usually cover general formations, creek drainages and major trails. Thus they only provide an overview of the forest. They are not detailed enough to determine elevations or topography or an accurate determination of distance. They are adequate for trip planning and selecting possible routes. But do not rely on them for on the ground reconnaissance.

Before a hike, read and study your map to know the trail and lay of the land. Look for prominent landmarks, including unusual shaped peaks and valleys, and for waterways and their direction of flow. Knowing the distance and the topography or contour of the landscape will help determine the difficulty of a hike.

A compass is another essential hiking tool. It is easy to become disoriented in the wild, and a compass will help regain navigating skills. But proper knowledge and skills are needed first to be able to read and orient actual locations with those positions on a map. Most compasses—and there are various types and styles—come with instructions. Know how it works prior to venturing out on a major expedition.

Using a compass and map may be further complicated by

the slight difference between true or map north (grid north) and compass north (magnetic north). It is important to know the magnetic variation, This is usually is found on the bottom of most topographical maps. For Jackson Hole, the variation presently is 15° to 15.5°. This variation can change, due to a natural shifting in the magnetic field. It is necessary to subtract this variation from your bearing to determine true north and alignment to a map. Many older maps still have out of date variations, usually around 17°. This 2° difference is critical.

Another, newer, electronic tool is the Global Positioning System (otherwise known as GPS). They are generally handheld, battery-operated units weighing about a pound. They continuously track and update their position through links to the GPS satellites and can provide a location within 100-300 feet.

Knowing the direction in which you are heading is an important aspect of navigation; this is called being "woods wise." If you do not have a compass or a GPS, it still is possible to keep a bearing on your location by following an appropriate course in relation to the sun and by triangulating with prominent landmarks. But, most important, maintain a sense of where you are and where you are headed at all times.

PERMITS—ASKING FOR PERMISSION TO EXPLORE

A backcountry permit is needed to camp in backcountry zones. These zones are specific delineated areas in canyons or meadows. Within a zone a finite number of campers are permitted. Although it is hoped that not all backcountry permit holders within a zone will end up camping next to each other, it is a possibility. What does happen, though, is that the prime locations along stream banks or lakeshores become overused and this has been the main problem with this system.

Within zones no fires are allowed. Portable cook stoves and cook kits are best for preparing food and water. Sanitation is another concern. In some of the more popular zones like Cascade Canyon pit toilets are available, but in other locations it is

a major problem. Mainly for this reason do not drink untreated stream or lake water. Filter or sterilize all surface water before consuming.

Backcountry permits are available at most of the ranger stations, some entrance stations and visitor centers—primarily Colter Bay and Moose—during regular business hours. Backcountry permits all are processed at Moose, and other offices call there to reserve space. Canoes and other watercraft also require permits (for a fee) and are available at the same locations. Mountaineering or climbing permits, however, are available only at Jenny Lake.

PLANNING EITHER A
SHORT OR AN
EXTENDED TRIP IS
ESSENTIAL TO AVOID
THE PITFALLS OF
UNFAMILIAR
TERRAIN.

Backcountry permits usually are made a day or two in advance, in person. But permits for institutional groups or individual reserved camping must be made by letter (and a fee) months in advance. When asking for a permit, have a specific destination in mind. Once a trail has been selected, review the backcountry office's area maps or handouts—these show the location of the zones and the statistics for each zone. When choosing a selection of camping zones, choose alternative sites as well, because first choices may already be booked. If trail information is needed, always be leery of the source; Quiz the backcountry-permits representatives to establish that they have hiked the trails. Often, such personnel are new to the area and have no local trail knowledge.

Camping in the surrounding national forests is an easier and less regimented process. The campsites—literally anywhere one can put a tent or sleeping bag—are available on a first come-first serve basis and a permit is not needed. Most of the backcountry has numerous sites that are equipped with fire rings and locating one—rather than constructing a new ring—is the preferred method.

While a camping permit is required for Grand Teton a fishing permit is needed for either the park or forest. Because Grand Teton National Park was established after Wyoming statehood—unlike Yellowstone National Park—Wyoming state jurisdiction and laws apply in Grand Teton. This jurisdiction includes fishing permits and regulations. The best place to obtain a Wyoming fishing permit and good fishing information is from the fish and tackle departments at the general stores throughout the park or the outdoor shops in Jackson.

TRAILMARKERS—A WORD OF CAUTION

Much of Jackson Hole's nearly 1,500 miles of trails are networked in an intricate web that are hidden from view to most visitors. Trailheads and trails usually are obscurely marked, if marked at all along the side of the road. A small, simple sign reading "…Creek" to denote its geographical name generally is all that marks the start of a trail. It is best to know a trail's approximate location on the road and to look for turnouts or small service roads in the vicinity. Some National Forest Service trailheads will have a trail board displaying "warning material" and a map, but most trailheads will not have any signage. This also is true for most National Park Service trailheads. But in either case the trails are usually indicated by their geographical place name.

When leaving a vehicle at a trailhead—try not to if it can be avoided—try to leave it as empty as possible. Thousands of cars left at trailheads have been broken into and looted over the years. The vandals often are professionals and break windows or locks to get at valuables—usually cash and cameras. Do not leave any valuables in sight or give the appearance of hidden valuables.

Every attempt has been made to check and recheck mileages given in this book by using aerial photogrammetry techniques and field surveys. But it will become evident that these mileages conflict greatly with National Park Service and National Forest Service trail signs that list mileages and distances.

During this author's lifetime of hiking Jackson Hole's trails, trail logbooks have been kept to record activity at front and backcountry trail signs. What becomes apparent when checking over these records are the inconsistencies and errors in trail mileages marked on those signs. With the exception of just short trails, most signs were found to have errors, and some mileages were grossly off—by as much as 70 percent. For a hiker in the field, relying solely on these trail signs is not only frustrating, but also dangerous. Do not rely on trail signs; instead, use good route-finding judgment, develop a sense of distance by studying maps, and, above all, be woods wise.

THINGS THAT BITE—BLOODSUCKING CREATURES

One of the most annoying trail hazards of Jackson Hole and Grand Teton are bloodsucking insects. Most of these belong to the insect order Diptera, or flies, and they include mosquitoes, horse and deer flies. These insects have evolved modified mouthparts for piercing, sucking and feeding on blood from a variety of hosts, including mammals, birds and even sugary secretions of plants. Thankfully most of these insects are attracted to their hosts for relatively short feeding periods.

Most of the bloodsucking Diptera, or flies and mosquitoes, are females. Two main forms of feeding are known. Pool feeders pierce or abrade the skin, then suck up the blood that exudes from the wound. This feeding form primarily is used by horse and deer flies. The other method, used by mosquitoes, is more specialized and takes the form of vessel feeding, in which a stylet-like structure pierces the skin and probes until its tip encounters a capillary. In some mosquitoes, their saliva inhibits coagulation of the host's blood. They then engorge themselves until abdominal stretch-receptors indicate a full meal. In mosquitoes, a blood-meal is followed by the maturation and deposition of eggs.

It is not clearly understood why insects are attracted to their hosts at specific seasons and times of the day. But wind conditions, light, temperature and humidity may be control-ling factors. Some appear to find their hosts by sight or move-ment (not color), but others depend on receptors to sense car-bon dioxide, warm convection currents, or body odors with specific chemical substances, such as lactic acid in mammals.

THE MOSQUITO IS A PERSISTENT SUMMERTIME PEST.

In Jackson Hole, the primary season for mosquitoes is early spring to midsummer, though this season can be extended in wet years. There are nearly 20 species of mosquitoes, which thrive at different times. Large snow mosquitoes are the first to emerge in spring, followed by small, more aggressive spe-cies that are common through the remainder of the season. Mosquitoes are very common in wet, wind-protected areas in small meadows, woods and their respective edge that inhabits wildlife. Temperature, wind and humidity generally control mosquito activity and numbers which increase on calm, over-cast days, early mornings or late evenings.

THE ROCKY MOUNTAIN WOOD TICK IS A COMMON SPRINGTIME PEST.

Biting flies present problems from July until the first heavy frosts in late August or early September. They are very com-mon in warm, wet, sedge-rush meadows and horse trails throughout the park.

Ticks are the other well-known bloodsuckers of Grand Teton. Even though they are not insects and are more closely related to spiders and other arachnids, they are small eight-legged, flattened, tough-skinned bloodsuckers that produce a puncture wound by use of a toothed beak. Ticks can transmit several diseases to humans. In 1975, Lyme Disease was identi-fied on the East Coast but no known case has originated from this region. Rocky Mountain Spotted Fever and Colorado Tick Fever has been known here since the 1930s. Both of these, how-ever, are extremely rare, with less than one known case of Rocky Mountain Spotted Fever per year in the United States.

After hiking in tick-infested country, conduct tick checks before going to bed at night. In Grand Teton and Jackson Hole, ticks generally are found in high wildlife-concentration areas, especially in the Gros Ventre Range and along elk migration routes originating from the National Elk Refuge in the spring.

HORSE FLY.

Tick populations appear to be dependent upon a number of factors, including temperature, humidity and the availability of host animals. They have been discovered in the valley as early as February and as late as October, depending on climatic conditions. But the tick season usually peaks from late April to late June, disappearing with drier, warmer weather.

Ticks usually find their hosts by climbing grass blades or shrubs and holding onto their perches with their hind legs while using their front legs as receptors for temperature (and perhaps chemical, light and dark) stimulations produced by their hosts. They cling to their passing host by using their forelegs to catch animal hair or clothing (especially dark-colored clothing). They then move to a suitable site, usually the scalp, hairline or sites of tight restrictions in clothing, especially the waistband and in socks. A simple body check at the end of a day of hiking should be effective in locating ticks.

If an embedded tick is discovered, it is not a serious concern. There are, however, several methods for removal. If the tick embedded recently, it might be persuaded to "pull out" on its own. The best procedure is to place a drop of alcohol on the tick (or even coat it with nail polish). This essentially blocks its breathing and gas exchange and irritates the parasite to remove itself. This method seldom works, though, and the match method only produces a burnt tick.

The most effective procedure is to remove the tick carefully with forceps by grabbing the head area, not the abdomen. Then cause the bite area to bleed slightly and clean the wound thoroughly with alcohol. Monitor the bite afterward for soreness, hardness or redness until it is cleared.

WILDLIFE—ENCOUNTERS IN THE WILD

By nature wild animals are not aggressive and usually avoid humans. But animals can become aggressive if they are provoked, teased, approached too closely, or if their young appear threatened or become separated. Most injuries resulting from human/animal encounters can be prevented simply by keeping a safe distance.

Many people consider bears to be the utmost danger on the trail. Bears, though, historically have effectuated few maulings or deaths, and most of these incidents have occurred in more recent years. When asked what to do when encountering a bear on the trail, I refer to what *Of Wolves and Men* author Barry Lopez told me: "I would meet the grizzly with how I lived my life." This is very appropriate advise. If people lived their lives in curiosity, their encounters likewise would be curious. But if people lived their lives in fear, their encounters would be frightful.

GRIZZLY CUB.

Regardless, it is best to first take precautions to avoid close encounters with bears. Many hikers believe that noise will help prevent a close encounter by warning bears of human presence and giving them ample time to detour. These techniques include talking, singing, or even attaching "bear bells" to packs while hiking in known bear territory.

To know if it is bear territory always be on the lookout for telltale bear signs along the trail. Bear signs include tracks, droppings and diggings. Tracks of adult grizzlies tend to be very large and distinct, with long claw marks projecting far ahead of the pad print. Black bear claw marks, on the other hand, are close to the pad print, if they show at all.

BLACK BEAR.

Bear droppings occasionally are found along many backcountry trails. Their freshness is relatively easy to judge, helping hikers determine whether the bear's presence was recent.

Grizzlies have large humps over their shoulders, made up of strong muscles used for digging. Their long claws are used for raking the soil in search of corms and tubers, and occasionally for digging up small mammals.

While most believe that grizzlies are the culprits in the majority of bear related injuries, black bears can be equally as dangerous—especially when it comes to sloppy, unkept camps. Make sure all food and packs are properly cached, hung high enough in trees so that bears cannot reach them.

GRIZZLY BEAR.

All bears are especially agile and can climb trees and gnaw through nylon cords. They can even understand the use of a rope holding hanging food in a tree. The best way to handle storage is to suspend food stuff, including cosmetics (soap, suntan lotion, lip salve, toothpaste, etc.) and their associated wrappers, between two trees, away from overhanging limbs—and

always away from the sleeping area. It should be suspended at least ten feet above ground and at least five feet away from tree trunks.

Another method is the counterbalance system with no tie-off points. This system uses two stuffed trash bags with the contents equally weighed and the bags attached at opposite ends of an approximate 10 foot cord. This apparatus then is slung over a branch, a cord or a pole strung between two trees. The bags can be adjusted and balanced using a stick. Again, the distances should be the same, ten feet above ground and five feet away from tree trunks. These are not foolproof methods for keeping bears at bay, but they should keep bears away from the sleeping area.

PROPER CAMP FOOD
STORAGE HELPS
PREVENT BEAR
DISTURBANCE.

Other than suspending food material from trees or limbs a small plastic barrel can be used to deter bears from pilfering. These small, beerlike barrels can store food and fit into a backpack and at night they simply lie on the ground. If a bear does try to ransack camp the seamless barrels are slippery enough to withstand the claws, teeth and weight of a bear and slide around without revealing its contents. However, because of its shape it can easily be lost, rolled, or moved a great distance by a hungry bear kicking it around while trying to break in.

Besides bears, two other trails animals have proven their ferociousness. Bison may appear to be lethargic and slow-moving, but they can run at speeds of 35 m.p.h., twice that of man. With speed, bulk and sharp horns, they are formidable adversaries. Moose, too, may have a gangly, awkward appearance, but when cornered in tight, narrow trails with no means of escape, their hooves, weight, strength and tenacity can prove dangerous. Always be alert to wildlife signs and potential hazards.

GRAND TETON'S REVENGE—WATER AND WATER PURIFICATION

For years, hikers and backcountry enthusiasts drank water directly from Grand Teton's streams and lakes. Every freshwater spring along a dry trail was well-known and marked on many of the early maps. These springs even became landmarks around which camps were established. But times have changed. The influx of people and the heightened awareness of harmful internal organisms has changed our drinking water habits.

Jackson Hole sits on the headwaters and drainage of the Snake River and, for the most part, its mountain water is pure and clean. But other factors have raised caution to drinking unpurified water. The National Park Service has pumped raw, unprocessed sewage into the streams and lakes. Even domestic water supplies were known to bear Hepatitis A, a viral infection with which thousands of visitors were infected. Many of those visitors, at home in distant lands, became jaundiced months later, not knowing where or when they were infected.

Another inherent problem discovered in the late 1970s was that giardiasis—also known as traveler's diarrhea—inhabits most of the lakes, streams and cold springs in the region. It is not known whether this organism is naturally present in the waters, has been carried by animals or, as some have speculated, by world travelers.

The giardiasis microorganism is borne as a cyst in swift moving, cold mountain water. It is ingested by a host animal—chipmunks, moose, bears or humans, for example—where it settles into the lower digestive tract and begins to reproduce and multiply. The protozoan *Giardia lamblia* causes severe inflammatory, intestinal disorders resulting in diarrhea, cramps and nausea. The symptoms generally do not appear until several weeks after infection takes place.

The best way to prevent these infections is to treat water, and there are several safe and reliable methods for doing so. One of the best ways is to boil drinking water for at least one minute, preferably up to 10 minutes. On long extended hikes most hikers boil enough to supply their needs for the coming day while preparing an evening meal. This way the water cools overnight and is palatable.

Other methods include chemical treatment. A number of commercial chemical treatments are available, but a tincture of iodine is the most common. It is available in liquid or tablet form, is generally messy, turns water pink, and has a distinct iodine taste. This is an essentially effective treatment but iodine water should not be consumed for prolonged periods.

One of the safest, easiest and certainly most convenient water-treatment methods involves use of portable water filters. They are available in three basic filter forms—paper (or glassfiber), charcoal and ceramic—which vary widely in price and quality. The only item of concern is that the filters must have a form of prefilter to reduce large particulate matter—sand, silt and other particles—from clogging the filter system and rendering it ineffective. Also, a filter system should have a pore size of 0.2 microns or smaller to filter out giardiasis cysts, cryptosporidia, and bacteria. And always be careful to follow the manufacturer's recommendations for cleaning and maintenance to prevent recontamination of your purified water.

Whatever treatment method is selected, it is important to drink clean water constantly while hiking, preferably keeping a handy water bottle to sip from at all times. Our bodies cannot store water and our need for water is driven by temperature, metabolism and exertion. During hot summers, Jackson Hole days under the sun absolutely require water to reduce risk of dehydration. Always drink enough water to ensure that urine remains clear. Cloudy or colored urine indicates the need for increased water consumption.

WALKING ON WATER—CROSSING THE IMPERILING ABYSS

Water crossing and other water-related activities are a high cause of Grand Teton deaths. Throughout the park's history, numerous deaths have been attributed to drowning.

For hikers, all water is potentially dangerous, especially if it is fast moving. Many of Grand Teton's and the surrounding forests stream crossings have some type of footbridge, ranging from log-trussed bridges to boardwalks or makeshift downed logs. But there are many times when no adequate crossing is available without getting wet feet and a stream fording is necessary.

Before venturing out on a hike, always plan stream crossings. In Jackson Hole, spring and early summer streams usually are swollen, and snowmelt and runoff are extremely dangerous. Know the season, streams and terrain before heading out, and prepare in advance. It is wise to take along an old, extra pair of sneakers or sport sandals to use in icy, cold water and on slippery, cobbled streambeds. It is not advisable to wear hiking boots, especially leather ones, for crossing. After a water crossing, cold, wet boots will only invite wet, squeaking feet and possibly blisters. Wearing shorts—in warm weather, loose-legged pants that can be rolled up—or even stripping down to one's underwear is preferable to becoming wet and risking hypothermia, the dangerous condition whereby the body temperature drops below 95°F (35°C). It is, therefore, important to remain dry and warm after a stream crossing.

When approaching a stream ford, assess your situation. Scout a good distance up and down the stream for a bridge or natural crossing and, if that is not available, a well-used fording site. Check the opposite bank for steepness and overhangs. Next, assess the lay of the stream or river and the appearance of the water surface for clues to hidden hazards. Standing waves can indicate a swift current over submerged rocks, debris, snags or tangled fallen trees. These should all be avoided.

BRIDGES HAVE BEEN CONSTRUCTED FOR CROSSING POPULAR STREAMS. BUT FEWER EXIST IN THE REMOTE BACKCOUNTRY.

After an assessment of the stream and a change into proper footwear and leggings, make certain that loose clothing, including bulky sweaters and jackets, are removed and tucked away into a pack. Do not buckle the pack's waist belt, and, if possible, put only one arm through its shoulder strap.

Use a pole or a stout branch as a third, supporting "leg" while crossing, especially if you are alone. The pole can be used to probe the bed for rocks or holes and to increase balance and stability. All told, use good judgment and, if the stream appears too hazardous, leave it for another day when it has subsided to a safe level.

BICYCLING—TWO WHEELING IN THE PARK

For such a large valley with nearly 1,500 miles of trails and additional miles of road, there are plenty of opportunities for bicyclists.

Bicycling does, however, have an early history in the valley. Early climbers in the valley brought velocipedes and Penny-Farthings, or ordinaries, to cruise the rutty, dirt roads during summer.

Today, the situation has changed. The narrow roads are extremely dangerous for cyclists during peak summer months. And all Grand Teton National Park backcountry trails are off-

BICYCLING IN GRAND TETON NATIONAL PARK.

limits to bicyclists. Within Grand Teton National Park superintendents have been historically livid and vehemently opposed to establishing bicycle access, paths or improved road conditions. As a result, few paths are available in the park. But the town of Jackson has developed a bike path that connects outlying residential and developed areas. This extensive path system is a safe alternative to highway shoulders.

Other areas available for biking, especially mountain biking, are Forest Service lands. In most instances, except designated wilderness, all trails are open and available for biking.

Some of the best trail rides are described in more detail in the individual trail descriptions, but an overview of paved areas available for road and mountain bikes include: The Buffalo Valley road, Jenny Lake loop, Antelope Flats road, Jackson-Aspen bike path, Fish Creek road and South Park bike path or loop. For additional mountain biking on rougher dirt or gravel surfaces, there are more possibilities, including: the Reclamation road, Shadow Mountain, Gros Ventre road, Curtis Canyon, Elk Refuge road, Flat Creek Ranch, Cache Creek, Putt Putt, Cache-Game Creek, Moose-Wilson road, Phillips Canyon, Black Canyon, Mosquito Creek and North Fork Fall Creek-Coburn Creek loop.

CANOEING—PADDLING THE BACKCOUNTRY

As with bicycling, canoeing is extremely restricted in Grand Teton. Only Jackson, Jenny, Leigh and Two Ocean lakes and the Snake River are open to canoeing. All other water passages are closed by the National Park Service.

The larger lakes and primary rivers—Jackson and Two Ocean lakes and the Snake River—that are open constitute the most dangerous and treacherous waters. If a canoe does capsize, survival time is limited in the icy waters. It is said that life is limited to 15 minutes for a man and 18 minutes for a woman before hypothermia begins.

In planning a canoe trip, allow ample time for weather and wind. In general, these lakes usually are calm and passable before 10 a.m., then winds begin to pick up during midday, and calm again by evening. But beware, local and regional storms can alter these conditions. The safest plan, even on calm waters, is to hug the shoreline. Never cross a large, open body of water, even though it may save time. Unpredictable winds can whip up three- to four-foot swells that easily capsize or swamp low gunnel boats. Always be certain to hug the shoreline and point your bow into waves.

One of the best and certainly the most interesting canoe trip is the String Lake to Leigh Lake excursion. To reach the starting point, unload and launch boats at the String Lake picnic area.

An early morning departure is necessary to avoid strong winds, which pick up speed as they move across Leigh Lake. The String Lake portion of this trip is ideal for children since most of the water is only calf- to knee-deep and the water does have an opportunity to warm up in this shallow stretch.

At the inlet to String Lake, or the outlet of Leigh Lake, is a series of rapids that must be portaged. This short tenth of a mile portage accesses Leigh Lake near Boulder Island. From there canoeing possibilities are unlimited on Leigh Lake, including lakeshore campsites.

Another great canoeing trip is Oxbow Bend. This trip begins at the outlet of Jackson Lake dam on the Snake River. Shortly after the dam the river wanders through a large bend or oxbow. This slow moving section of river is ideal for canoeing, and the Oxbow is well-known for its wildlife viewing. Usually beaver, muskrat, and white pelicans are present. Occasionally moose, elk, bald eagles, great blue herons, loons, trumpeter swans or river otters make their appearance too.

SKIING—MOVING ON SNOW AND ICE

Jackson Hole has some of the finest cross-country and telemark skiing opportunities available. Its deep, powdery snow and mountainous terrain, provide ideal conditions for any imaginable trip.

But Jackson Hole and Grand Teton does have extremely cold winters. Temperatures have been recorded at minus 65°F, and it is not unusual to have stretches of several weeks to months in which the temperature remains below 0°F. Usually the week between Christmas and New Year's, and into early January peaks as some of the coldest. Some of the best skiing or snowshoeing occurs in late winter or early spring, when daylight hours are longer, snow is plentiful, and temperatures are more moderate.

The outside park road (U.S. highway 26/89/191) leading to Flagg Ranch or over Togwotee Pass is the only road into Grand Teton that is plowed during winter. All other roads within the park are snowbound but are accessible by oversnow vehicles, including snowmobiles. Other roads leading into the valley include Snake River Canyon, Hoback and Teton Pass. They are usually open, but can close due to climatic conditions.

Tracked ski trails are limited to popular ski routes. These are primarily from Colter Bay, Cottonwood Creek (leading to Bradley & Taggart lakes or Jenny Lake), Brooks Lake, Shadow Mountain, Cache Creek and Teton Village. But backcountry skiing opens every imaginable possibility. Teton Pass is one of the more accessible and popular locations for backcountry skiing, as well as from the summit of Snow King Mountain.

PIONEER SKIING IN THE TETONS.

Snowshoeing, likewise, can launch from these same areas. Because of the maneuverability of snowshoes, treed or forested areas can provide interesting excursions where skis have difficulty maneuvering.

Before venturing out during winter, always be certain that you are prepared for all extremes and all conditions. Crossing snow on skis or snowshoes requires skill and hard work. Make sure you have all necessary equipment or spares, including extra clothing, food and water, as these items may not be available at the trailhead. Most important, know your limitations, abilities, distances and topography before heading out on a long trip. *Do not count on help or rescue*; it may never come. Always consider yourself on your own and take appropriate precautions.

HIKING FLAGG RANCH

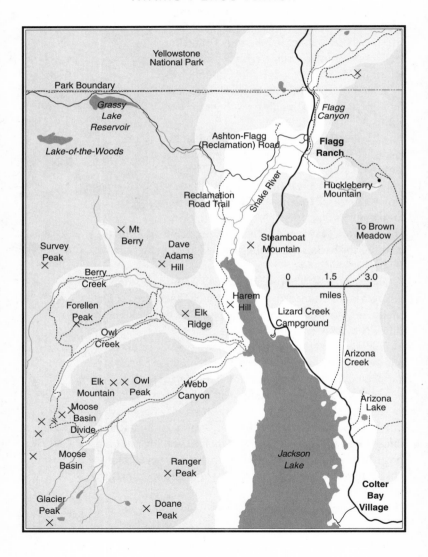

Yellowstone
National Park

Park Boundary

*Grassy
Lake
Reservoir*

Lake-of-the-Woods

Flagg
Canyon

**Flagg
Ranch**

Ashton-Flagg
(Reclamation) Road

Reclamation
Road Trail

Shake River

Huckleberry
Mountain

× Mt
Berry

Dave
Adams
× Hill

Survey
Peak
×

Berry
Creek

Forellen
Peak
×

Owl
Creek

× Elk
Ridge

Harem
× Hill

Steamboat
× Mountain

To Brown
Meadow

Lizard Creek
Campground

0   1.5   3.0
miles

Elk × × Owl
Mountain   Peak

Moose
×× Basin
× Divide

Webb
Canyon

Arizona
Creek

Arizona
Lake

×

Moose
Basin

×

Ranger
× Peak

*Jackson
Lake*

**Colter
Bay
Village**

Glacier
Peak
×

× Doane
Peak

FLAGG RANCH

Flagg Ranch territory is known as "no mans land." It is defined as the region between southern Yellowstone and northern Grand Teton national parks. Neither park claimed the territory during their origin. As a result it was omitted and the region did not even show up on most official maps. In 1972 Congress corrected this oversight by authorizing a strip of Forest Service land along both sides of the highway to connect Yellowstone and Grand Teton. This corridor became John D. Rockefeller Jr. Memorial Parkway. In legislation it is a separate unit of the national park system, but is administered by the National Park Service at Grand Teton National Park.

THE NORTHERN TETON RANGE.

This region is remote even by western standards. Other than the operations at Flagg Ranch there is no human habitation within a 20 mile radius. It is, however, the home of grizzly bears, wolverines, harlequin ducks and Snake River cutthroat trout.

The topography also is just as varied. On the western edge of this region the northern end of the Teton Range tapers into the Yellowstone Plateau, buried beneath ancient volcanic debris. While the eastern side is bordered by low mountains of the Huckleberry Ridge. Between the two ranges the Snake River emerges from its headwaters in Yellowstone and sidles down the center of the valley. At first the river races down Flagg Canyon where it then emerges at Flagg Ranch. It then becomes a tranquil meandering river amidst willow flats before it enters Jackson Lake reservoir.

Within this headwater of the Snake River are a number of hiking possibilities. Some of the more remote trails require a canoe trip across Jackson Lake before trails loop into and out of Teton canyons. Other trails follow the rim of Flagg Canyon or wander up to old fire lookouts or high country meadows where graves mark the resting spot of early explorers.

But for its wildness away from the beaten path this region of Jackson Hole cannot be surpassed.

FLAGG CANYON TRAIL

Length: 2.5 miles, one way.
Elevation change: Trailhead at 6,910 feet (116-foot loss).
Trailhead: Located at the south entrance to Yellowstone National Park. Just a few hundred feet south of the entrance sign is an unmarked road leading east to a picnic area and boat launch.

The Flagg Canyon Trail on the upper Snake River is a little-known yet highly interesting trail along the cliff-like embankment of the Snake River. It is primarily a fishermen's and floaters' access used by guests at nearby Flagg Ranch, but its unusual terrain and scenery rank it as one of Grand Teton's best hikes.

The hike begins at the picnic area, boat launch and trailhead, located a few hundred feet south of the Yellowstone National Park boundary sign. Most of the hike is through lodge-

YELLOW-BELLIED
MARMOT.

pole forest along the western shore of the river. Most of the hike involves crossing downfallen trees. But it is a rewarding trek, providing plenty of vantage points overlooking the river.

Along the first half of the hike, the river is in a narrow gorge. At about the halfway point, it becomes even more restricted by large, angular boulders, but the water in some areas is very tranquil. On hot summer days, boaters often tie up along this stretch of river and take icy-cold dips to cool things off. This is one of the more scenic stretches of the river.

DUNCECAP
LARKSPUR.

Also about halfway through the hike, a cutoff trail junctions with the river trail. This short access leads to the highway and a small unmarked parking area that is used primarily by fishermen to access the river.

Shortly beyond the midway point, the river leaves the canyon and the terrain opens up. Near the end of the trail, the river bends sharply west and the trail exits at the Flagg Ranch bridge.

Just across the road is the old Flagg Ranch site. The family owned lodge burned to the ground during a winter in the early 1980s. Thereafter, the owners were hounded by the National Park Service, which claimed the tract was located on a 100-year floodplain, and pushed to relocate. By 1995, a new lodge designed and sited by the National Park Service was cut out of and built on 20 acres of pristine forest north of the old site. The new site, lacking proper access and design, nearly drove the business into bankruptcy. That and the death of the owner prompted its sale in 1997.

During this process, the National Park Service requested and received nearly $13 million for development of its own facilities, including further development and construction of the Park Service compound at Moose, on a floodplain located directly on the shore of the Snake River.

RECLAMATION ROAD TRAIL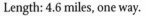

Length: 4.6 miles, one way.
Elevation change: Trailhead at 6,940 feet (260-foot gain).

Trailhead: Located on the Reclamation Road (Grassy Lake Road or Ashton-Flagg Road), 4 miles west of Flagg Ranch. The last stretch of road parallels the Snake River, then turns sharply west, away from the river. It is about a mile to the trailhead after leaving sight of the river. The trailhead is an unmarked small parking area on the south side of the road.

The Reclamation Road Trail, also known as the Glade Creek Trail, is a primary access—especially by horse—into the northern Teton Range. It is the only land access, on the east side of the mountains, to this region. Other, longer trails do, however, reach from the Idaho side of the range into the remote recesses.

This trail connects with the Berry Creek Trail (see Berry Creek Trail for description), Owl Creek Trail (see Owl Creek Trail for description) and Webb Canyon Trail (see Webb Canyon Trail for description). Most of these trails originate at the Berry Creek cabin on the shore of Jackson Lake, and if you choose not to make a water crossing of Jackson Lake, the Reclamation Road Trail provides an alternative route.

From the roadside parking area, the trail heads south into dense a lodgepole forest. It cir-

MONKSHOOD.

cumvents a small knoll to the east and follows Glade Creek to the Snake River bottom. The trail then fords Glade Creek and continues following the willow river bottom to Jackson Lake.

Just after Jackson Lake, the trail begins to leave the shore to circumvent another knoll—Harem Hill. At this point, the trail meets the Berry Creek Trail to head west, or continues south between Elk Ridge and Harem Hill to the Berry Creek cabin. The junction area is a triangle of cutoff trails, along with several parallel horse trails that avoid stream crossings, so it can be a bit confusing. Use your sense of direction and your route-finding skills.

Berry Creek cabin is situated near the bank of Berry Creek

before its confluence with Jackson Lake. The cabin is somewhat hidden by a fringe of trees, but numerous trails and paths lead to the cabin. During most of the summer, a National Park Service backcountry ranger is stationed here, so the cabin should show signs of occupancy.

From here, the trail junction leading to either Owl Creek or Webb Canyon trails is just a quarter of a mile west.

BERRY CREEK TRAIL

Length from Berry Creek cabin to:

Harem Hill	1.6 miles, one way.
Reclamation Road Trail junction	2.75 miles, one way.
Hechtman Lake spur trail junction	6.0 miles, one way.
Survey Peak spur trail junction	8.0 miles, one way.
Berry Creek (upper) patrol cabin	8.4 miles, one way.
Owl Creek cutoff trail junction	8.5 miles, one way.
Jackass Pass	10.4 miles, one way.
Conant Pass	12.6 miles, one way.

Elevation change: Trailhead at 6,779 feet (821-foot gain to Berry Creek upper patrol cabin and 2,032-foot gain to Conant Pass).
Trailhead: Access to Berry Creek Trail is possible either by boat across Jackson Lake via Lizard Creek, or by trail via the Reclamation Road Trail. Either way the trail begins at the Berry Creek cabin.

SHOWY GREEN
GENTIAN.

This gem of the north country is an isolated, yet a historically busy byway to and from Jackson Hole. Native Americans on their summer pilgrimage to Jackson to fish the lakes, hunt game and collect berries, used this trail primarily from Idaho over the mountains via Jackass or Conant pass.

Later, early explorers, outlaws and settlers used the same trails into the valley. By 1910, with the raising of Jackson Lake reservoir, the water inundated that stretch of the Conant Trail, rendering it useless. If Jackson Lake were not dammed, Conant Pass or Jackass Pass likely would have become a major highway leading in and out of the valley.

ELK THISTLE.

Remnants of the old Indian/trapper/settler trails still are visible today in the upper headwaters of Berry Creek. Most are faint trails, but the parallel and crisscrossing old horse trails can confuse things.

To reach the trailhead, cross Jackson Lake by boat, or hike from the Reclamation Road and merge with the Berry Creek Trail. For those who cross the lake by boat, the trailhead is located directly across, or west, of Lizard Creek campground—also known as Fonda Point. It is possible to launch a small boat there, especially a canoe. This area of the lake is made up of dangerous open water and should be treated with respect. Do not try to cross if the water is choppy or it is windy. The best times to cross are before 10 a.m., or in the evening. During those times, winds usually are calm and the lake is tranquil. The crossing is just 0.8 miles, but in a canoe it always seems farther. Before casting off Lizard Point, find and fix a prominent landmark due west and aim for it. When you reach the opposite shore, there is a small bay to the south. The first creek is the inlet of Berry Creek, which also marks the trailhead.

HAREBELL.

The other access is a land route from the Reclamation Road (see Reclamation Road Trail for description). This route is 4.6 miles due south of the Reclamation Road and junctions with the Berry Creek Trail.

The trail begins at the Berry Creek cabin, at the mouth of Berry Creek, as it enters Jackson Lake. The cabin is somewhat hidden by a fringe of trees, but it is the prominent landmark, and most trails and paths lead to it. During summer, a backcountry ranger takes up residence there and, on occasions, uses the nearby Moose Basin Divide and Berry Creek patrol cabins.

From the Berry Creek cabin, the trail heads north between two ridges—Elk Ridge and Harem Hill—and veers north of Elk Ridge. Interestingly enough, Berry Creek runs along the west and south side of Elk Ridge, so the trail does not connect with the creek again until the northwest edge of Elk Ridge. From here, the trail begins to enter Berry Creek canyon.

Once the trail parallels the creek, the area becomes very

marshy, including a series of beaver dams and the resulting series of small ponds behind them. For the most part, the trail circumvents the wet, marshy areas, but be prepared for a number of stream crossings and wet feet. This drainage can be extremely dangerous in June. Spring runoff swells the creek and creates sponge-like meadows until subsiding by early July.

The ponds and stream are, however, well-known for fishing—especially for their brook trout. Harlequin ducks, brightly colored and patterned, also nest along the stream. These ducks prefer fast-moving mountain streams and isolation. If you spot any, give them a wide enough berth, as this is one of the last nesting areas and refuge for these locally rare ducks.

The upper patrol cabin is just above the ponds, along the creek. The mountain to the northwest of the cabin is Survey Peak (9,277 feet). There is a spur trail to its summit—a 1,677-foot climb—and the junction is less than a half mile back down the trail.

STICKY GERANIUM.

On the hillside south of the cabin, on the north face of Forellen Peak (9,776 feet), is an abandoned asbestos mine. Tailings and old machinery are found in the vicinity, but the mine was never a commercial success. The spot also was used by Indians, who obtained soapstone (talc) for pipes, and other utensils.

From the patrol cabin, you can continue due west to Jackass Pass (8,470 feet) on the park boundary. This historical trail branched from here in several directions. The most common route leads past Hominy Peak (8,362 feet) and down the Hominy Creek drainage into Idaho. Another trail heading south from Jackass Pass leads to Conant Pass (8,811 feet), also on the park boundary.

Another option from the upper patrol cabin is to head south on the cutoff trail to Owl Creek. This trail is not maintained. It is fairly distinct, but confusing, up to the divide between Berry and Owl creek drainages. From the divide down to Owl Creek, the trail is steep and very faint toward the bottom, so route-finding may be necessary. If you use this cutoff trail, you can return to Berry Creek cabin down Owl Creek drainage (see Owl Creek Trail for description).

OWL CREEK TRAIL 🌲 〰️

Length from Berry Creek cabin to:

Berry Creek cutoff trail junction	3.4 miles, one way.
Forellen Peak cutoff trail junction	6.3 miles, one way.
Moose Basin Divide	10.4 miles, one way.

Elevation change: Trailhead at 6,779 feet (2,941-foot gain).
Trailhead: Access to Berry Creek Trail is possible either by boat across Jackson Lake via Lizard Creek, or by trail via the Reclamation Road Trail. Either way the trail begins at the Berry Creek cabin.

The Owl Creek-Moose Basin Divide-Webb Canyon trail makes for one of the more popular backcountry, overnight trips in Grand Teton National Park. Its unique access—the crossing of Jackson Lake—also adds a sense of adventure to this remote and intriguing area.

To reach the trailhead at Berry Creek cabin, take a boat across Jackson Lake, or hike the 4.6-mile trail from the Reclamation Road (see Reclamation Road Trail for description). If a boat is chosen to cross the lake, the best launching point is Lizard Creek campground, but Leeks Marina or Colter Bay also are options if a motor-propelled boat is used. Otherwise, the 0.8-mile crossing from Lizard Creek can be done by canoe. If you launch at Lizard Creek, head due west. When you reach the shoreline, you'll find a small bay to the south. In the bay, the first inlet is Berry Creek and the southern stream inlet is Moose Creek. Beach the craft west of Berry Creek, in a protected area. Berry Creek cabin is about a quarter mile up the creek, a little off the bank and somewhat hidden by a fringe of trees. Most of the paths and trails lead to the cabin, which is usually occupied by a National Park Service backcountry ranger during summer.

Past the cabin and another quarter mile upstream is the

junction for Webb Canyon (Moose Creek) and Owl Creek trails. The southern trail fords the raging Moose Creek and the northern trail heads into the steep canyon bordered on the north by Elk Ridge.

By the 3-mile mark, the trail enters a marshy, moose-haven meadow. In early summer, this area is nearly impossible to cross without getting into at least ankle-deep water or muck.

At the marsh, Owl and Berry creeks merge, with Berry Creek entering from the north. The trail fords the stream here, where a 1.2-mile cutoff trail is found leading north to Berry Creek.

After entering the Owl Creek drainage, it is still a little marshy. But by mid-July to mid-August, large stalks of blue-flowering, tall larkspur line the trail in dense patches.

After the marsh area has been passed, the looming mountain to the north is Forellen Peak (9,776 feet), which once held a Forest Service lookout. To the south are the twin peaks of Elk Mountain (10,612 feet). The gully running down Elk Mountain points to a gully that runs up, opposite Owl Creek, to Forellen Peak. It is unmarked but is the best location to access the Berry Creek and Owl Creek divides.

THE RUGGED REGION SOUTH OF WEBB CANYON.

Keep a sense of direction in tact while bushwhacking. Head up this gully; about halfway up, a number of faint trails become visible. Forellen Peak once was a well-used Forest Service lookout, and a number of utilitarian trails lead to and from the peak to the divide and other points. At the same halfway point, you can follow the contours west to the divide and a well-used visible trail, which heads down into Berry Creek (see Berry Creek Trail for description), and other prominent landmarks. From the divide, another trail leads to the summit of Forellen Peak.

From the junction to upper Owl drainage, the trail becomes faint as it crosses barren exposed limestone. Along the divide, a series of cairns mark the trail, which then drops into Webb Canyon (see Webb Canyon Trail for description).

WEBB CANYON TRAIL ▲ ≋

Length from Berry Creek cabin to:

Moose Basin patrol cabin	7.8 miles, one way.
Moose Basin Divide	9.8 miles, one way.

Elevation change: Trailhead at 6,779 feet (2,941-foot gain).

Trailhead: Access to Berry Creek Trail is possible either by boat across Jackson Lake via Lizard Creek, or by trail via the Reclamation Road Trail. Either way the trail begins at the Berry Creek cabin.

WESTERN TOAD

WESTERN CHORUS FROG

WESTERN SPOTTED FROG

LEOPARD FROG

Webb Canyon, also known as Moose Creek, is a popular remote backcountry trip. It is similar to its sister canyons to the north. The Owl Creek to Webb Canyon loop, especially, is one of the best in the park. This 20.2-mile trip reaches into deep recesses of the northern Teton Range.

The beginning of the Webb Canyon trip, like Berry Creek or Owl Creek trails, begins with either a boat trip across Jackson Lake via Lizard Creek campground, or a hike south from the Reclamation Road (see Reclamation Road Trail for description). Either way, the trailhead begins at the Berry Creek cabin.

A quarter mile beyond the Berry Creek cabin is a major stream crossing. At this point also is the junction to Owl Creek. But from here the Webb Canyon Trail heads south and crosses Berry Creek. This is a raging stream, especially from late May to early July. The ford usually is calf- to knee-deep by mid to late summer. Exercise caution while crossing this stream, even during low season; several people have drowned here.

From the crossing, the trail enters Webb Canyon. At first, it is an open, relatively flat meadow. But then the trail begins a steep climb as the canyon closes in. Moose Creek drains the largest watershed in the Teton Range, and this stream is a swift mountain torrent. Luckily, it requires only two moderate and a few minor tributary fordings, located higher up the canyon before Moose Basin.

Webb Canyon was named in honor of Dr. Seward Webb. He was a member of the 1879 Carrington expedition on a reconnaissance to determine if the boundary of Yellowstone National Park should be extended to include the Teton Range. This proposal was defeated, but the range was later incorporated into a national park in 1929. Only the mountains, however, and not the lakes at their bases or even Webb Canyon, were included in the original incorporation. It was not until 1943 that the valley was included, forming the Jackson Hole National Monument. The two then were joined in 1950 to form Grand Teton National Park.

In the canyon is Johnny Graul's mystery mine, which he slowly chiseled into the solid gneiss and granite bedrock over a period of 23 years. It is still unknown what he was mining.

Just before Moose Basin is Moose Creek Falls, a small cascade that tumbles from Moose Basin. From there, the trail climbs via a large switchback to the large open Moose Basin. The expansive basin, made up of thin soil covering limestone bedrock, was highly polished and sculpted by glaciation.

A small patrol cabin is perched and exposed in the middle of the basin, and the trail passes by it. From the cabin, the trail continues through sparsely treed meadows to Moose Basin Divide, then drops into Owl Creek (see Owl Creek Trail for description).

HUCKLEBERRY MOUNTAIN TRAIL

Length from Sheffield Creek Trailhead to:

Huckleberry Mountain junction	5.0 miles, one way.
Huckleberry Lookout spur trail	5.8 miles, one way.
Brown Meadows	6.8 miles, one way.
Bailey Meadows	10.6 miles, one way.
Arizona Creek Trailhead	14.5 miles, one way.

Elevation change: Trailhead at 6,900 feet (2,715-foot gain to lookout, but an overall gain of 1,415 feet to Brown Meadows).

Trailhead: Located a few hundred feet south of the Flagg Ranch bridge on the east side of the highway. This is the Sheffield Creek Trailhead, and it is about a quarter mile drive to the end of the dirt road.

Huckleberry Mountain is a less-popular hike, mainly because it is not in the Teton Range. But this hike into Teton National Forest provides a tour of the regeneration of the 1988 fires, an ascent to a fire lookout, and a descent to a busy and historical meadow.

A tourist camp was located at Sheffield Creek Trailhead at the turn of the nineteenth century. Hunting guides Ed and Ben

Sheffield sold goods and provided accommodations here before the road was condemned by the government for construction of the Jackson Lake reservoir.

The trail starts in the aftermath of the 1988 Huckleberry Fire, during which most of the forest along the trail was burned extensively. Now only blackened and stark skeletons of the forest remain. But coming up among the skeletons are patches of fireweed and young lodgepole pines. The fire opened up the forest and likewise the vistas.

ELK ANTLER ALONG
THE TRAIL.

At the start of the trail is an uphill climb through burned forest to Huckleberry Ridge. At the top of the ridge, the trail crosses into Teton Wilderness and is at the base of one of the two summits of Huckleberry Mountain. The trail then continues around the peak and junctions on the east side of Huckleberry Mountain. This mile spur trail leads to the southern summit, where there is a fire lookout.

Huckleberry Mountain lookout is a historic structure and one of the first prefab buildings in the valley. The walls were built in panels and horse packed up the mountain for reassembly at the summit. Today, the lookout is used occasionally but usually is boarded up.

From the lookout, the trail descends the east side of Huckleberry Ridge returning to the junction. From there the trail continues to Brown Meadows. This is a very historic meadow, as well as a crossroad into the wilderness. This four-way junction has trails leading west to Bailey Meadows and Arizona Creek (see Arizona Creek Trail for description), south to Wildcat Peak or Pilgrim creek (see Pilgrim Creek Trail for description), or east along Rodent Creek.

The meadow itself has been a popular site for poachers or "tuskers," and a small cabin—along the western edge of the meadow—burned in the 1988 fire. Originally the cabin may have been built for "tuskers" purpose. Other cabins, mainly well hidden ones, are scattered throughout the area. The meadow also is a popular camp and horse-picketing site. The grave of Thomas Brown, whose body was discovered here in 1891, is marked on the eastern edge of the meadow.

MONARCH
BUTTERFLY.

HIKING COLTER-BAY

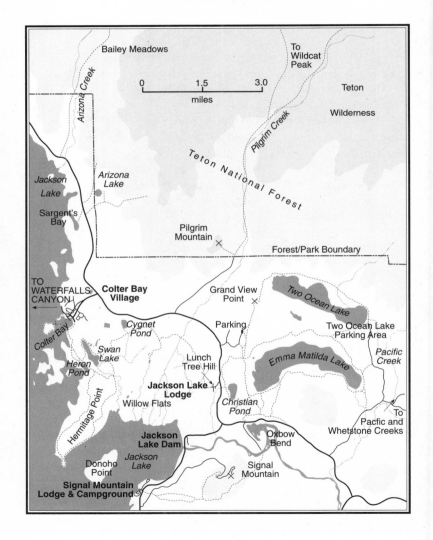

Bailey Meadows

To Wildcat Peak

Teton

Wilderness

Arizona Creek

0   1.5   3.0
miles

Pilgrim Creek

Teton National Forest

Jackson Lake

Arizona Lake

Sargent's Bay

Pilgrim Mountain ✕

Forest/Park Boundary

TO WATERFALLS CANYON

Colter Bay Village

Grand View Point ✕

Two Ocean Lake

Colter Bay

Cygnet Pond

Parking

Two Ocean Lake Parking Area

Pacific Creek

Swan Lake

Heron Pond

Lunch Tree Hill

Emma Matilda Lake

Hermitage Point

Jackson Lake Lodge

Willow Flats

Christian Pond

To Pacific and Whetstone Creeks

Jackson Lake Dam

Oxbow Bend

Jackson Lake

Donoho Point

Signal Mountain ✕

Signal Mountain Lodge & Campground

COLTER BAY-JACKSON LAKE LODGE

Only a few locations within Jackson Hole offer the convenience of numerous and a variety of hikes originating from one location as does Colter Bay or Jackson Lake Lodge. It is the Picadilly Circus of Grand Teton National Park and everyone and everything seem to pass by or through here.

Jackson Lake dominates the region with its 25,000 acres of water surface and 17 mile length. But when explorers first entered this valley in 1871 they discovered a different lake in a different form. By the early turn-of-the-nineteenth-century Idaho potato farmers were experiencing floods and drought. In spring their fields were inundated and by August the same fields turned to dust, a typical western summer. The farmers followed the Snake River into Jackson Hole and built an earthen dam at the site of the present dam. This impounded water allowed the Snake River to be regulated, holding runoff water in spring and releasing extra water during the drier summer months.

MOUNT MORAN
FROM OXBOW
BEND.

43

Since then the reservoir level has risen by several successive new dams over the years, and the original Jackson Lake level is now 38 feet below the current height.

Within this diverse landscape dominated by a lake and a mountain range is a full spectrum of choice hiking trails. Many of the trails wander among lodgepoles, climb to overlooks for impressive views, lead to waterfowl covered lakes, while others, follow stream, river or lake shores for tranquil, peaceful walks. Still others lead to waterfalls, rare geologic fossils or wildlife meadows.

ARIZONA CREEK TRAIL

Length from Arizona Creek Trailhead to:

Bailey Meadows   3.9 miles, one way.

Brown Meadows   7.7 miles, one way.

Elevation change: Trailhead at 6,845 feet (1,470-foot gain to Brown Meadows).

Trailhead: Located about 4.8 miles north of Colter Bay junction. Just past Arizona Creek bridge is an unmarked service road, which heads north about 0.3 miles to an old corral hidden in the trees.

Arizona Creek has long been a historical trail into the wilderness. Poacher or "tusker" cabins were scattered along the trail and throughout the area. Today, this trail is used primarily to access Teton Wilderness and regions beyond. Because it is a long-distance destination trail, most wilderness excursions begin from here on horseback.

The trail from the corrals and parking area leads due north, following an old road to the ford of Arizona Creek. Just a little more than a half mile from the ford, the trail enters Teton Wilderness, then veers away from Arizona Creek and ascends to Bailey Meadows. The trail then meets up with the creek again, fords it again, and continues into Brown Meadows.

GREAT BLUE HERON.

Brown Meadows is a popular campsite and a crossroads

to other regions. To the north is the Sheffield or Huckleberry Mountain Trail (see Huckleberry Mountain Trail for description), which leads to Huckleberry Lookout and emerges at Flagg Ranch. To the east is the Rodent Creek Trail, and to the south is Whetstone Creek—known for its fossilized dinosaur footprints—and connecting trails to Pilgrim Creek.

ARIZONA LAKE TRAIL

Length: 1.2 miles, one way.
Elevation change: Trailhead at 6,910 feet (40-foot gain).
Trailhead: The turnoff to the trailhead is 2.5 miles north of the Colter Bay junction. The unmarked, narrow dirt road is on the east side of the highway. It is the first turnoff going north from Colter Bay. At the end of this short half-mile road is a small parking area.

This path is along the road but is relatively unknown, primarily because its trailhead is well-hidden. The short spur road leading to the trailhead is unmarked and appears only as a narrow dirt track leading into the forest.

A road once lead to Arizona Lake, but since then it has not been maintained. Most of the road has grown in and is now covered with deadfall. The trail, however, follows this old road and downed trees must be maneuvered.

HOLLY HOCK.

From the trailhead, the route leads east up a small canyon to a ridge overlooking wetlands. This ridge is on the park boundary, and the lake itself is in Teton National Forest. The trail fords the marsh, skirting the eastern edge to the small lake.

Arizona Lake was named for "Arizona George," who wintered on Arizona Creek during 1888-89 and later was found dead along the creek.

PILGRIM MOUNTAIN TRAIL

Length: 1.8 miles, one way.

Elevation change: Trailhead at 6,977 feet (1,297-foot gain).
Trailhead: Located on the Pilgrim Creek road. The turnoff for this road is 2.4 miles north of the Jackson Lake Lodge junction. One and a third miles up the dirt Pilgrim Creek road is a spur road that heads due north. The half-mile spur road dead-ends at the base of Pilgrim Mountain.

This hike and bushwhack up Pilgrim Mountain provides unusual views of Jackson Lake and the Teton Range. It is a seldom-hiked peak without an official trail. But it is relatively easy to ascend and achieves a different perspective of the region.

From the trailhead at the end of a half mile two track is the base of the mountain. This spur road, can, at times, be

OXBOW BEND AND
MOUNT MORAN.

blocked by the National Park Service. The stretch between the base of the mountain and Pilgrim Creek road can be accessed from any location along the road. The unmarked trail essentially heads up through patches of open hillside and Douglas firs. The summit features two points, nearly equal in height, though the northern point has been declared the summit at 8,274 feet.

From the top are wonderful views of Two Ocean and Emma Matilda lakes. Between the two lakes is a rounded knoll known as Grand View Point (see Grand View Point Trail for description). To the south is Jackson Lake Lodge, and to the west is Jackson Lake and Mount Moran. This is the same vantage point that explorer and photographer William H. Jackson recorded them in 1878.

PILGRIM CREEK TRAIL ▲

Length from Pilgrim Creek trailhead to:

Wildcat Peak trail junction	3.0 miles, one way.
Rodent Creek pass	7.0 miles, one way.

Wildcat Peak	9.5 miles, one way.
Brown Meadows	12.7 miles, one way.

Elevation change: Trailhead at 7,109 feet (2,584-foot gain).
Trailhead: Located on the Pilgrim Creek road. The turn-off for this gravel and dirt road is 2.4 miles north of the Jackson Lake Lodge junction. The trailhead begins at the end of Pilgrim Creek road and the trail leads beyond the buck-and-rail fence.

SWALLOWTAIL
BUTTERFLY.

This Teton Wilderness trail begins at the boundary of Grand Teton National Park at the end of the Pilgrim Creek road. It leads up into the wilderness and connects with the Teton Wilderness network of trails. This trail, like other Teton Wilderness trailheads, is a gateway for extended trips and it is not unusual to find horse packers—but to a lesser extent—coming in or departing from here.

The trail for the first section follows Pilgrim Creek, criss-crossing it several times in the lower section. Some of these fordings can be avoided, but others are inevitable. The valley opens up to an impressive scope, with the creek bottom lined with dense, heavy willows. Grizzly bears frequent this creek bottom and their tracks often can be seen in the muddy banks along the creek.

About three fourths of the way up the open valley the trail junctions. It is confusing in this area. An old trail once headed up a western tributary of Pilgrim Creek and is shown on many maps. But it has not been maintained and has since overgrown, especially with the occurrence of forest fires. Just beyond the confluence of that tributary is the main junction that leads to Wildcat Peak. The Pilgrim Creek trail, however, does continue following the stream to the northeast.

The Wildcat trail leaves the stream bottom and heads north through spotted forests and meadows to a divide separating Pilgrim Creek from Rodent Creek. At this pass the trail follows the ridge line west to the highest peak, Wildcat (9,693 feet). This is, however, a steep, rugged cross-country climb.

From Wildcat are wonderful views of the Teton Range and Jackson Lake at their feet. The trail does connect via a circuitous route to Brown Meadows (see Huckleberry Mountain Trail for description). This trail, like the loop trail connecting to Pilgrim Creek, is unmaintained and in poor condition.

SARGENTS BAY TRAIL

Length: 0.25 miles, one way.
Elevation change: Trailhead at 6,810 feet (38-foot loss).
Trailhead: This unmarked parking area is about 2.9 miles north of Colter Bay junction. The distinguishing characteristic here is the small phantom pond across the road to the east that fills during early summer and dries up as the season progresses.

Sargents Bay is a short, but popular trip for Colter Bay residents. It accesses Jackson Lake and is a popular fishing spot.

From the parking area, the trail heads down a small gully to the bay. It follows an old wagon road, possibly the Old Military Highway, which was in place before development of the Jackson Lake reservoir between 1910 and 1916. Before the dam, the lake level was nearly 39 feet lower, and Sargents Bay did not exist. The road led to Marymere, John Dudley Sargent's log lodge. In 1890, Sargent—related to artist John Singer Sargent—and his partner, Robert Ray Hamilton—a relative of Alexander Hamilton—built an impressive ten-room lodge, 22 feet by 70 feet, on a knoll overlooking Jackson Lake.

BLACK BEAR.

A year later, Hamilton drowned while crossing the Snake River, but his body was not discovered for 12 days. His family, fearing foul play or the possibility that the recovered body was not Hamilton's, had the remains exhumed and shipped back to New York for positive identification.

Sargent's Jekyll-and-Hyde temperament brought him before the public on several occasions. In 1897, soldiers skiing from Yellowstone heard a woman's scream coming from the lodge, but got no response when they knocked. They later reported the incident in Jackson, and concerned residents returned to Marymere to find Mrs. Sargent badly beaten "while Sargent, steeped in the fumes of opium and morphine, calmly awaited the moment of her death." They took the woman by sled to Jackson, where she died a few days later. But before her death, she told the story of repeated beatings and the assault on one of their young daughters. After her death, the couple's five children were sent to live with relatives in the East. A vigilante committee formed, but Sargent disappeared. Two years later, he turned himself in at Evanston and was tried and acquitted. In 1906, he remarried, and his second wife occasionally was seen wandering naked through the forest, often sitting in a tree near the lodge sunbathing or playing her violin. Eventually, she returned to a mental institution in New York. Sargent, lonely and shunned, committed suicide in 1913 and is buried on the point. Marymere was torn down in the 1930s, and an even larger lodge of 5,200 square feet—the AMK (Berol) Ranch—was built just south of the original lodge site. The ranch now is used by the University of Wyoming as a field research station.

Since the raising of the reservoir and the formation of the bay, the old Marymere site is on a spit of land, and the graves are isolated in the center of the point. The shore along the bay is stony and rocky, but not so much that you can't explore here.

WATERFALLS CANYON COUNTRY.

WATERFALLS CANYON TRAIL

Length from Jackson Lake shore to:

Columbine Falls	2.2 miles, one way.
Wilderness Falls	2.6 miles, one way.

Elevation change: Trailhead at 6,769 feet (1,751-foot gain to the brink of Columbine Falls and 2,651-foot gain to the brink of Wilderness Falls).

Trailhead: Access to Waterfalls Canyon begins at Colter Bay marina; a boat is needed to cross Jackson Lake to access the mouth of the canyon.

Waterfalls Canyon, especially its approach, is one of the more unusual hikes in Jackson Hole.

To begin, cross Jackson Lake by boat. Waterfalls Canyon is directly west across the lake from Colter Bay marina. Several options are available for crossing the 4 miles of open water: You can rent a canoe or small motor boat at the marina, though boat wranglers there do not recommend straying more than a quarter mile from shore in a canoe, which precludes their use for this hike. A small motor boat and extreme caution are the best solutions. Early morning and evening are the best and

THE GRAND TETON
FROM THE NORTH
COUNTRY.

calmest times to cross this large, open body of water. Midday winds increase and usually form choppy or whitecap waves. If a rental boat is not opted for another possible way to cross is by a scenic boat excursion (for a fee). During the summer these ply the lake regularly throughout the day. The scenic boat trips usually include drop offs to some of the trailheads, but this is highly unpredictable as policies and shoreline conditions can change. Most of the shoreline is stony, with few sandy points to beach a boat.

From the mouth of Waterfalls Canyon, a faint trail wanders up the canyon. This is not a highly used or maintained trail and, in places, disappears. A keen sense of direction and good route-finding skills are essential, as is scrambling in some places. The canyon and mountainside burned extensively during the 1974 Waterfalls Canyon Fire. The standing skeletons of the forest still remain, but thick brush and shrubs have grown up in the more protected moist areas of the canyon.

The canyon is narrow and steep, and the first visible falls

usually are Wilderness Falls, the upper of the two waterfalls. A sharp turn in the canyon then reveals lower Columbine Falls. Both are in rugged, glaciated terrain and are two of the best waterfalls in the park. A scramble is necessary to circumnavigate the 200-foot Columbine Falls to continue up the canyon to the base of 265-foot Wilderness Falls.

COLTER BAY NATURE TRAIL

Length: 1.5 mile loop.
Elevation change: Jackson Lake shoreline at 6,772 feet (Little or no elevation change).
Trailhead: Begins directly behind Colter Bay visitor center.

This easygoing trail begins just behind (north) of the Colter Bay visitor center. It follows the Colter Bay shore and crosses a bridge to a small island, then makes a loop around the island along the Jackson Lake shoreline and returns to the visitor center. This short, evening stroll provides a superb view of sunsets behind Mount Moran and Jackson Lake.

MOUNT MORAN.

SWAN LAKE AND HERON POND TRAIL

Length: 2.0 mile loop
Elevation change: Trailhead at 6,780 feet (no perceptual elevation change).
Trailhead: Follow the paved road south from the Colter Bay visitor center toward the marina.

No other trail in Grand Teton National Park ranks higher than this one for an early morning hike.

Numerous unmarked trails exist in this area. Most are interconnecting horse trails but others are access roads or trails to water systems, sewage-processing ponds, power lines or maintenance sheds—either active or abandoned. Finding the correct trail often can be frustrating; your sense of direction and route-finding skills are essential here.

FIREWEED.

Stay primarily on trails leading left (unless you are starting from the cabin area, then take trails leading right), or as indicated on signs. The old sewage-settlement ponds are located about half a mile in, on the right side of the trail, and consist of several shallow ponds split by dividers. Under right wind conditions their scent is unmistakable.

Swan Lake is down the hill and beyond the old sewage pond. The trail follows the western shore of Swan Lake, then loops back by connecting with Hermitage Point Trail (see Hermitage Point Trail for description). The return route passes Heron Pond and generally follows the shoreline of Jackson Lake.

A number of different routes are formed using horse trails and shortcuts. A trail also follows the east shore of Swan Lake. It crosses a dense willow thicket, known for its resident moose, at Third Creek and connects with the Hermitage Point Trail.

During winter, these peripheral trails become obscure, so cross-country skiers generally use only the main trails. The loop to Swan Lake and Heron Pond is considered one of the primary winter ski trails in Grand Teton National Park. Winter wildlife here is limited, though. Moose, swans and other waterfowl using the lakes during summer migrate to other locations during winter. Even beavers, active during summer, are either nestled in their lodges or actively retrieving stored food under ice. The most common winter bird life found here are mountain and common chickadees.

THIMBLEBERRY.

HERMITAGE POINT TRAIL

Length: 8.8 mile loop.
Elevation change: Trailhead at 6,780 feet (no perceptual elevation change).
Trailhead: Begins at the southern end of the Colter Bay park-

ing area, near the boat ramp—or can be accessed from the cabin area.

If you have hiked the Swan Lake Trail as an early morning hike, this is a good trail to continue on for an afternoon hike. It also is one of the best cross-country ski trails for an all-day ski excursion.

The first section of the trail can be confusing. Several horse trails crisscross this area, as do roads, trails to sewage-treatment plants, water and electrical maintenance buildings. So route-finding and a sense of direction (or maybe Hansel-and-Gretel-style bread-crumb trails) may be necessary.

The trail skirts Heron Pond and Swan Lake (see Swan Lake and Heron Pond Trail for description) and loops south around the tip of a peninsula, wandering through lodgepole pine, sagebrush openings and lakeshore vistas.

LUNCH TREE HILL TRAIL
Length: 0.2 miles, one way.
Elevation change: Trailhead at 6,851 feet (84-foot gain).
Trailhead: The trail begins in front of the Jackson Lake Lodge picture windows.

Lunch Tree Hill provides an unimpaired view of the Teton Range, but it also is saturated in park-creation history. This short trail makes for a popular after-dinner stroll for guests staying at the lodge.

The trail begins in front of the Jackson Lake Lodge's Willow Flat overlook. From here, a paved trail heads north to the summit of a small knoll—Lunch Tree Hill. The self-guided trail loops around on the summit and returns to the porte cochere of the lodge. The sagebrush-covered summit provides a panoramic view of the entire Teton Range, from the southern end of Jackson Hole to the high Yellowstone plateau in the north.

This little hill was the historic site of a picnic stop used by Yellowstone National Park superintendent Horace M. Albright in 1926. Up until then, Mr. Albright had been unsuccessful in his attempts to incorporate the Tetons into Yellowstone's borders, or even protect the valley of Jackson Hole. But in 1926, when John D. Rockefeller, Jr., along with his wife and three sons, came to Yellowstone for a visit, Albright took them to Jackson Hole, and they stopped at this spot for a picnic lunch. Rockefeller was sullenly quiet, but he was immediately impressed by the grandeur of the mountains. He quietly returned to New York and wrote to Albright, asking him to draw a map and estimate the cost of private land in the valley.

By 1927, Rockefeller formed the Snake River Land Company, a front to keep landowners from asking exorbitant sums from the multimillionaire. By 1930, the company owned most

of the private land on the valley floor—nearly 35,310 acres at a cost of about $40 per acre.

In 1929, three years after Rockefeller's visit to Jackson Hole, U.S. Congress enacted to protect the mountains of the Teton Range but not the valley or the lakes at its feet. By 1943, after years of unsuc-

MOUNT MORAN FROM THE AIR.

cessful attempts to donate his Jackson Hole land to the people, Rockefeller made a final decree. Either accept the land as a gift or it would be sold off in parcels. By this time, he had spent more in property taxes than he had on the actual purchase.

Rockefeller's threat prompted President Franklin Roosevelt to exercise executive authority to create the Jackson Hole National Monument, mainly from public lands, including national forest—but not the Rockefeller land. This presidential authority stirred Congress, but slowly. Not to be outdone by the president, the governing body skirmished over the national monument until 1950, when it passed a bill to incorporate the national monument as part of what now is Grand Teton National Park. This new park finally encompassed the Rockefeller lands and the valley we know as Jackson Hole.

CHRISTIAN POND TRAIL ▲

Length: 3.1 mile loop from the road.
Elevation change: Trailhead at 6,841 feet (no perceptual elevation change).
Trailhead: Located at the Christian Creek Bridge. There is not, however, ample parking at the bridge, so it is best to park at the gas station or start from Jackson Lake Lodge.

Christian Pond is a fun hike originating east of Jackson Lake Lodge. It traverses excellent wildlife habitat and early mornings hikers are rewarded with sightings of trumpeter swans—which often nest on the lake—as well as coyotes and moose.

The 3-mile loop trail begins at the Christian Creek Bridge. Take the trail to the north, as it provides the best views of the lake and wildlife. The trail undulates around the lake through a variety of habitats, including willow, marsh, sagebrush meadow and lodgepole-pine forest.

Other trails lead from Christian Pond Trail, including Grand View Point, and Two Ocean and Emma Matilda lakes (see respective hikes for description). Horse rides, also, lead from Jackson Lake Lodge to this small wildlife pond, making for numerous crisscrossing and confusing trails. Again, use your sense of direction to circumnavigate the pond.

GRAND VIEW POINT TRAIL

Length to Grand View Point from:
  Grand View Point Trailhead   0.75 miles, one way.
  Jackson Lake Lodge   2.4 miles, one way.
Elevation change: Trailhead at 6,885 feet (701-foot gain). Jackson Lake Lodge elevation at 6,841 feet (745-foot gain).
Trailhead: Accessed by one of two trailheads: 1) Drive 0.9 miles north of the Jackson Lake Lodge intersection to an unmarked eastward turnoff. Follow this dirt road for a half mile to a parking area and trailhead; 2) Begin at Jackson Lake Lodge.

SMALL-FLOWERED
PENSTEMON.

Grand View Point Trail has been a popular and traditional sunset hike to an overview of the Teton Range, Jackson Lake, and Two Ocean and Emma Matilda lakes.

Two trailheads access Grand View Point. One is a about a mile-long hike from the trailhead. The other is nearly three times longer and joins the same trails, but begins from Jackson Lake Lodge. Either route is enjoyable and provides wonderful views and insight into the area's natural history.

The route from Jackson Lake Lodge crosses under the highway bridge and heads north, passing by Christian Pond. Be aware that numerous horse trails crisscross this area, and they can be confusing; keep your sense of distance and location in tact here. After leaving a willow-lined valley, the trail heads into the Douglas fir and lodgepole forest.

THE TETON RANGE FROM GRAND VIEW POINT.

Eventually, the trail junctions with the Emma Matilda-Two Ocean trails, at a five-way split. The north trail continues on to Grand View Point, but be careful for another trail veers off to the access road to Grand View Point trailhead. Along the way are glimpses of Emma Matilda Lake.

After another three quarters of a mile, the trail junctions again, this time with the Grand View Point Trail. The remaining three quarters of a mile is a gradual climb through small meadows and scattered Douglas fir and lodgepoles.

At the point, a remnant of intrusive volcanism, are superb views of the Teton Range and Jackson Lake to the west, and Two Ocean Lake and plateau to the east. Because of the prevailing rising or setting sun, early morning light is the best for viewing the Tetons and evening light is best for Two Ocean views. The trail continues north, then east along Two Ocean Lake (see Emma Matilda and Two Ocean Lakes Trail for description) to the eastern shore and trailhead.

ARROWLEAF BALSAMROOT.

During summer, the point also is well-known for its wildflower display, especially arrowleaf balsamroot, and for the numerous butterflies that congregate there, especially yellow swallowtails and monarchs.

EMMA MATILDA AND TWO OCEAN LAKES TRAIL

Lengths to:

Emma Matilda Lake Trail from;

Jackson Lake Lodge	9.8 mile loop.
Two Ocean Lake parking area	10.3 mile loop.

Two Ocean Lake Trail from;

Jackson Lake Lodge	11.5 mile loop.
Two Ocean Lake parking area	8.5 mile loop.
Grand View Point trailhead	9.2 mile loop.

Elevation change: Trailhead at Jackson Lake Lodge is at 6,841 feet (a 59-foot gain to Two Ocean Lake parking area; 54-foot gain to Two Ocean Lake; and a 27-foot gain to Emma Matilda Lake).

Trailhead: These lakes can be approached from two directions. Access them either via Jackson Lake Lodge from the west or by driving 4.2 miles up Pacific Creek to Two Ocean Lake on the east side, where there is a parking area and trailhead. The Pacific Creek Road is located 3.8 miles east of Jackson Lake Lodge, or 1.2 miles west of Moran Junction.

TWO OCEAN LAKE FROM GRAND VIEW POINT.

For an easygoing, but long, day-hike, the Emma Matilda and Two Ocean Lakes Trail is a highly recommended series of interconnected loops and trails. A number of different routes can be linked to make for a short hike or a longer one that visits both lakes and Grand View Point. Basically, two main loop trails circle the two kidney-shaped lakes positioned one above the other in an east-west orientation. Both lakes can be reached from either Jackson Lake Lodge on the west side, or by driving up Pacific Creek on the east side.

From Jackson Lake Lodge Two Ocean Lake or Emma Matilda Lake is approached via a number of routes. A couple of alternatives are offered by way of Christian Pond (see Christian Pond Trail for description). One trail drops along the southern shore of the pond and crosses a low ridge to the southwestern shore of Emma Matilda Lake. From there the trail does connect into a network of hiking and horse trails. Another trail approaches and follows along the southern shore of Emma Matilda. A few others head south and connect to U.S. Highway 89-287, emerging at Oxbow Bend. Yet another heads due north leading to Grand View Point and beyond to Two Ocean Lake loop.

The other option from Jackson Lake Lodge is to head north of Christian Pond. This route leads to Grand View Point and Two Ocean Lake.

The last major approach from the west uses the Grand View Point trailhead (see Grand View Point Trail for description). Again, this is a good, short access to Two Ocean Lake.

The east side of the lakes is a more remote region, but the Pacific Creek road does dead-end directly at Two Ocean Lake. From the trailhead, one can venture along the north shore of the lake for the best views of the Teton Range, or head south toward Emma Matilda and connect with other trails there.

TWO OCEAN COUNTRY.

Emma Matilda Lake was named by William Owen, for his wife in the late 1800s, when Owen was a surveyor for the General Land Office. Two Ocean Lake received its name from the nearby Two Ocean Plateau, where waters split to opposite oceans. This lake, however, flows only to the Pacific Ocean.

Whatever approach or route is chosen, this area provides a quiet and secluded sanctuary. Even bears, including wandering grizzlies, find solace here. In August, 1994, an early morning jogger woke up a grizzly from its day bed alongside the trail. The surprised bear mauled the jogger before ambling off into the forest. Other evidence of bear activity can be found in the strip of land between the two lakes, where a few tree trunks display claw marks.

This area is especially tranquil during winter. The only appropriate accesses are by way of Christian Pond or by striking north from Oxbow Bend. But on the east side is a longer, more difficult approach. The last two miles of the Two Ocean Lake road, from the Pacific Creek road junction, is unplowed and adds two miles of skiing to reach the lake. This region is seldom skied, so tracks or paths are few; employ a sense of direction and route-finding skills.

PACIFIC CREEK TRAIL

Length from Pacific Creek trailhead to:

Whetstone Trail junction	1.2 miles, one way.
Gravel Creek Trail junction	3.9 miles, one way.
Enos Creek cutoff trail	8.3 miles, one way.
Enos Lake	11.0 miles, one way.
Pacific Creek/Enos Lake junction	12.8 miles, one way.
Two Ocean Trail junction	13.9 miles, one way.
Two Ocean Pass	14.6 miles, one way.

Elevation change: Trailhead at 7,048 feet (1,072-foot gain).
Trailhead: Pacific Creek trailhead is located 8.4 miles up Pacific Creek road. The trailhead is at the end of the road and the border of Teton Wilderness. The turnoff to the Pacific Creek road is located 3.8 miles east of Jackson Lake Lodge, or 1.2 miles west of Moran junction.

Pacific Creek Trail, also known as the Atlantic-Pacific Creek Trail on U.S. Forest Service maps, leads into one of the foremost and largest wilderness areas in the contiguous United States. This trail is almost a highway used to access points along the way, but it is primarily used to reach the heart of Two Ocean Plateau.

Along the first 4 miles to Gravel Creek junction, the trail heads up the relatively broad, open bottom land of Pacific

THE RUBBER BOA RESEMBLES A LONG PIECE OF SMOOTH MILK CHOCOLATE.

Creek. This is an easy section of trail, except for a few stream crossings, including Whetstone Creek, which can be treacherous in early summer and still very wide even in late summer or fall. But the stream crossing of Pacific Creek can even be more hazardous.

At the Enos Creek Cutoff Trail junction, the trail splits for 4.5 miles but later rejoins. The two alternate trails are about the same length. The north trail loosely follows Pacific Creek and junctions with the Mink Creek Trail. The southern route is more interesting because it passes by Enos Lake and junctions with a series of trails originating from Turpin Meadows, including Enos, Lava and Clear Creek trails (see respective trails for descriptions).

The trails join again on Pacific Creek and continue upstream. Just before Two Ocean Pass, Two Ocean Trail on the North Buffalo Fork (see Two Ocean Trail for description) meets this trail. Starting here, the terrain becomes marshy and boggy, with dense willow thickets. The terrain is so indecisive here that water along the Continental Divide is uncertain which direction to flow. Even cartographers had difficulty delineating a line for the Continental Divide, so they simply split the line to encompass a 5-mile strip that is one mile wide.

In the middle of this zone, called Two Ocean Pass, is the small headwaters of Two Ocean Creek. Even this water has difficulty determining which direction to flow. The stream splits, one branch forms Pacific Creek and heads to the Pacific Ocean, and the other, Atlantic Creek, flows toward the Gulf of Mexico. This is an unusual phenomenon and occurs in only one other location along the spine of the Rocky Mountains, that being at the Great Divide in Canada's Banff National Park.

From Two Ocean Plateau, one can head in almost any direction, but the most popular destination is Hawks Rest on the Upper Yellowstone River at the southern boundary of Yellowstone National Park. This area is known as the Thorofare Region of Yellowstone (see Thorofare Trail in *Hiking Yellowstone Trails*).

SNOWSHOE HARE.

WHETSTONE CREEK TRAIL

Length from Pacific Creek trailhead to:

Whetstone Trail junction	1.2 miles, one way.
West Trail junction	4.2 miles, one way.
Coulter Creek drainage	6.4 miles, one way.

Elevation change: Trailhead at 7,048 feet (1,354-foot gain to Coulter Creek Pass).

Trailhead: Pacific Creek trailhead is 8.4 miles up Pacific Creek Road. The trailhead is at the end of the road and the border of Teton Wilderness. Go 3.8 miles east of Jackson Lake Lodge or 1.2 miles west of Moran junction to reach the turnoff to Pacific Creek Road.

SPRING BEAUTY IS ONE OF THE FIRST WILDFLOWERS UP IN SPRING.

Whetstone Creek is an unusual area off the beaten path of Pacific Creek Trail. The area was the site of Whetstone Mining Company in 1895. The company was in search of gold, but never found the gold-bearing vein it had suspected. Until the 1990s, when dinosaur tracks were discovered in a steep, remote canyon, though, Whetstone Creek was relatively unvisited by humans.

This area also is well-known for its natural history. Whetstone Creek acts as a corridor for elk migrations to and from their higher summer pastures. Naturalists, including Olaus Murie and Smithsonian scientists, made early studies of elk habits along this drainage.

The Whetstone Creek Trail uses the Pacific Creek Trail for the first 1.2 miles, then branches off and heads due north along the base of Whetstone Mountain. The trail parallels Whetstone Creek but does not join it for about 3 miles, when the trail splits again. One trail, called the West Trail, heads west and leads up a fork of Whetstone Creek. But the east trail continues up the main fork of Whetstone Creek to the pass (8,402 feet), separating Whetstone and Coulter Creek drainages. The trail continues until it connects with the Pilgrim Creek Trail (see Pilgrim Creek Trail for description).

Hiking Togwotee Pass

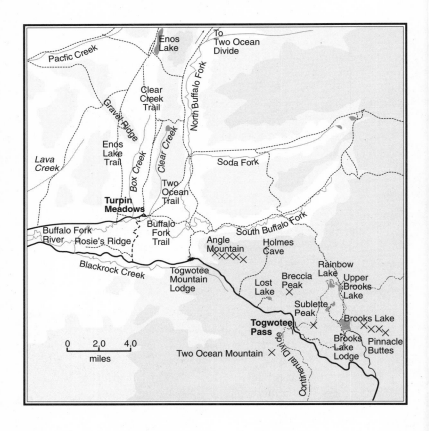

TOGWOTEE PASS

Togwotee Pass straddles the Continental Divide and cuts through and accesses one of the largest wilderness areas of the lower 48 contiguous states. It is true wilderness in the sense that it is unlogged, roadless, undeveloped and nearly undisturbed by the presence of man. It also is the last home and vestige of the few remaining grizzly bears in the United States.

Because this region straddles the Continental Divide its topography is varied and unpredictable. As streams decide on their path to the ocean unusual features form. One steam on its descent along the divide splits in two. Half of the streams water flows to the Pacific Ocean via the Snake River, while the other half heads toward the Atlantic via the Missouri and Mississippi rivers. It is an unusual phenomena that only occurs in a few spots on this continent.

TRUMPETER SWAN.

This region holds onto winter longer than surrounding lower elevations and snow comes early and prolongs into summer long after most areas are deep into their summer. Once snow has melted the harbingers of spring arrive late. But the catching up period is fast, as is summer at this elevation. The meadows come alive with the colors of wildflowers, and the movement of migrating and hibernating animals. Elk weave in and out of the meadows and forest and yellow-bellied marmots, pikas and ground squirrels add their chorus to the meadow melody.

DOUGLAS FIR.

Within the Togwotee Pass and Two Ocean Plateau are a number of challenging hikes, especially extended one way and loop hikes into the heart of the wilderness. Other hikes lead across scenic ridges, along rivers, hidden lakes, or to limestone caverns.

LAVA CREEK TRAIL

Length from Lava Creek trailhead to:

Wilderness boundary	0.8 miles, one way.
Lava Creek	3.9 miles, one way.
Enos Lake Trail junction	10.1 miles, one way.
Enos Lake	13.4 miles, one way.

Elevation change: Trailhead at 6,871 feet (944-foot gain).
Trailhead: The Lava Creek trailhead is on Buffalo Valley road, 1.9 miles east of Heart Six Ranch and across the road from Fir Creek Ranch.

This Two Ocean Plateau approach is the longest among the trails leading to Enos Lake. The other approaches include Pacific Creek, Enos Lake, Clear Creek and Two Ocean trails (see each for description). Like the others, Lava Creek Trail is another access into the Two Ocean Plateau and regions beyond via Enos Lake.

The first section of the trail—until it joins with Lava Creek—is dry. In this stretch, a spur trail junctions from Heart Six Ranch. At Lava Creek, the trail crosses the creek and follows the meadow and drainage to its headwaters and its divide. At the divide, the trail merges with the Enos Lake Trail.

From this area are good views of the 1987 wind sheer that leveled nearly 14,000 acres of lodgepole trees. The trail then again junctions with the Clear Creek/Divide Lake Trail just before Enos Lake.

ENOS LAKE TRAIL

Length from Box Creek trailhead to:

Wilderness boundary	0.6 miles, one way.
Gravel Ridge	4.8 miles, one way.
Lava Creek Trail junction	7.5 miles, one way.
Enos Lake	10.8 miles, one way.

Elevation change: Trailhead at 6,918 feet (897-foot gain).
Trailhead: The Box Creek trailhead is located on the Buffalo Valley road 1.8 miles west of Turpin Meadows.

The Enos Lake Trail is a favorite for local horse packers and outfitters as a gateway into Teton Wilderness. During summer months and especially in the Fall, pack strings of horses and mules depart from here laden with provisions for remote camps. The trail leads to a large backcountry lake set in a deep lodgepole forest. Trails within the region converge and diverge from here.

COWPARSNIP.

This trail is very similar to and even parallels the Clear Creek Trail (see Clear Creek Trail for description) to the east. The Enos Lake Trail is a dry trail with Box Creek drainage about a half mile east.

The trail climbs at first before somewhat leveling out and then wanders over post glacial deposits; remnant clays and gravels. After about 7.5 miles the trail junctions with the Lava Creek Trail (see Lava Creek Trail for description) before joining with a number of crossroad trails in the Enos Lake area. This trail, as with others, leads to Two Ocean Pass and continues on toward the Thorofare region of southeastern Yellow-stone.

Along the upper stretches of the trail the effects of a 1987 sheering wind with tornado-like results leveled nearly 14,000 acres of forest. The forest was composed primarily of lodge-pole pines with shallow root systems. This freak, high velocity wind toppled trees in one direction as if they were pickup sticks. This unusual occurrence, even though it is rare, has happened several times before in the Jenny Lake area and in the Madison Plateau of Yellowstone.

CLEAR CREEK TRAIL 🔺 🦌

Length from Clear Creek trailhead to:

Wilderness boundary	0.5 miles, one way.
Divide Trail junction	6.8 miles, one way.
Enos Lake	9.4 miles, one way.

Elevation change: Trailhead at 6,990 feet (825-foot gain).
Trailhead: Located on the Buffalo Valley road at Turpin Meadows. It is on a short dirt road just a mile north of the Turpin Meadows bridge.

Teton Wilderness, abutted with Yellowstone National Park and Washakie Wilderness, is one of the largest remote areas in the Lower 48 states, and the Clear Creek Trail involves the short-est and the most direct approach to its boundary. It is a rela-tively dry trail because it does not follow a creek drainage, but it does parallel its namesake stream which lies east by a half mile to one mile away.

The trail begins at the northern edge of Turpin Meadows and immediately begins climbing out of the meadow. Along the first half mile toward the wilderness boundary is a series of switchbacks, then the trail begins to level off somewhat, fol-lowing a broad ridge. Clear Creek is to the east and Box Creek is to the west.

Just before Clear Creek Lake the trail splits, but the two then parallel each other. The trails merge again near the small lake, set away from the trail to the east, with the Divide Lake Trail. The trail heading east junctions with the Two Ocean Trail (see Two Ocean Trail for description) after about a mile and a half, coming up the North Buffalo Fork. The northwest-trending trail continues on to Enos Lake.

Enos Lake (7,815 feet) is a large backcountry lake, about 300 acres in size. On the southern edge is a forest service patrol cabin. The lake is a popular layover and a crossroad for trails leading to Two Ocean Divide country and environs beyond. The primary trail leading past the lake is the Pacific Creek Trail (see Pacific Creek Trail for description).

TWO OCEAN TRAIL

Length from Turpin Meadows trailhead to:

Buffalo Fork trail junction	0.4 miles, one way.
Wilderness boundary	1.6 miles, one way.
Mud Lake	2.1 miles, one way.
Soda Fork Meadows	3.4 miles, one way.
North Fork Meadows	6.8 miles, one way.
Enos Lake spur trail	11.1 miles, one way.
Pacific Creek trail junction	12.4 miles, one way.
Two Ocean Pass	12.8 miles, one way.

Elevation change: Trailhead at 7,000 feet (1,120-foot gain).
Trailhead: The starting point for Two Ocean Trail is on the eastern edge of Turpin Meadows. A large parking area is complete with stock loading ramps and holding areas.

SAGEBRUSH BUTTERCUP.

Of all the approaches to Two Ocean Plateau, this is perhaps the most popular, mainly because it is the shortest and most scenic route. This trail also is used as the primary horse packing route into the remote regions of Two Ocean and Yellowstone's Thorofare.

The first three miles of the trail cuts across a bend of the Buffalo Fork River, through lodgepole pines, and connects with it again at Soda Fork Meadows. From the meadows northward, the trail follows the drainage all the way to Two Ocean Pass.

DEER FLY.

Because of its proximity to water, this trail is a haven for mosquitoes during most of the summer. And because of livestock, it's also a ideal conditions for biting flies.

Two Ocean Trail also provides the means to a network of interconnecting trails. Most are horse and pack trails leading to camps in the more remote regions of the wilderness. One such trail is the Soda Fork Trail, which leads east up Soda Fork drainage.

But Two Ocean Trail continues north, up the North Fork drainage and through North Fork Meadows. At the meadows, another trail junctions to Enos Lake, a crossroad for interconnecting trails and 3.4 miles off the Two Ocean Trail.

About a mile before Two Ocean Pass, the trail merges with Pacific Creek Trail (see Pacific Creek Trail for description). Again, Two Ocean Pass and Yellowstone's Thorofare are fascinating regions of exploration.

BUFFALO FORK TRAIL

Length from Turpin Meadows trailhead to:

Two Ocean Trail junction	0.4 miles, one way.
Wilderness boundary	1.0 mile, one way.
North Buffalo Fork River	2.9 miles, one way.

Elevation change: Trailhead at 7,000 feet (75-foot gain, but a 650-foot gain over a knoll).

Trailhead: The starting point for Two Ocean Trail is on the eastern edge of Turpin Meadows. A large parking area is complete with stock loading ramps and holding areas.

This is a wonderful short trail that explores the upper regions of the Buffalo River to the point where the north and south Buffalo Forks converge. For the most part, the trail follows the river, but on benches and hillsides above it.

For a short portion at its beginning, the trail uses the Two Ocean Trail (see Two Ocean Trail for description), before entering Teton Wilderness. At that point, the trail heads over a knoll, up and away from the river, then descends to the confluence of the north and south Buffalo Forks of the river. The North Buffalo Fork originates at Two Ocean Pass on the Continental Divide.

To continue on, a hiker must ford the North Buffalo Fork. From there, one trail continues east along the South Buffalo Fork and another heads due south, after another river crossing, for about two and a half miles, to Togwotee Lodge.

ROSIE'S RIDGE 🚴 🎿 🐎

Length: 4.6 miles, one way.
Elevation change: Trailhead at 7,862 feet (134-foot loss).
Trailhead: Located 5 miles east of Hatchet campground at Fourmile Meadow. The access is 0.3 miles off the highway on the dirt Turpin Meadows road. The two-track trail begins on the western edge of the meadow.

Rosie's Ridge is an easygoing hike, mountain bike or winter ski to a prominent point overlooking Buffalo Valley. Even though it is a ridge with a steep embankment dropping to the Buffalo River floodplain, the trailhead actually begins at a higher elevation and descends shallowly to the point.

WOOD'S ROSE.

Rosie's Ridge is very prominent when approaching by vehicle. At the Hatchet Motel or Blackrock Ranger Station, it is the steep slope to the north, with the highway skirting its southern slope.

It was named in honor of Rudolph "Rosie" Rosencrans, who—in 1903—became the first forest ranger in what then was Yellowstone Park Timber Reserve. He built a log cabin at the base of the ridge, near the river. The cabin has since been moved and now rests at the Blackrock Ranger Station.

Rosencrans was born in The Tyrol region of Austria and graduated from Vienna University. He moved to Jackson Hole in 1903. By 1908, the Yellowstone Timber Reserve became the newly established Teton National Forest. But by the late 1920s, Rosencrans left Blackrock because of his failing eyesight. He died in Jackson in 1970.

The trail along the ridge is really a two-track, and this road provides access to radio towers and transmitters at the point.

The road may or may not be open to vehicle traffic but is open to foot traffic and provides a wonderful stroll through meadows, lodgepole and aspen stands. The two-track parallels the highway about 500 feet above it.

At the point are unsurpassed views of Buffalo Valley, the river meandering through the willow bottomland in the foreground and the complete span of the Teton Range in the background.

HOLMES CAVE IN THE EARLY DAYS.

For winter skiing, the Turpin Meadows road is not plowed and is closed to vehicle traffic—except snowmobiles—to Turpin Meadows Lodge. Skiers can park near Fourmile Meadow picnic area, across from the junction in a plowed parking spot, and ski in from there. This route adds just 0.3 miles to the one-way distance.

HOLMES CAVE TRAIL

Length: 4.2 miles, one way.
Elevation change: Trailhead at 8,780 feet (820-foot gain).
Trailhead: A short access road off of state highway 26/287 marks the trailhead. This is 4.9 miles west of Togwotee Pass, or 4.1 miles east of Togwotee Lodge.

Holmes Cave is an unusual feature on the edge of Teton Wilderness. Even though it was discovered in 1898 and has been a popular hiking destination there is no delineated trail to the cave. A good portion of this faint trail involves route finding.

From the trailhead at the end of a short access road the trail heads northeast to a saddle in the southern end of the Angle Mountain ridge. This ridge line marks the wilderness boundary. Below the saddle is a large meadow and a tree-fringed lake. Holmes Cave lies a half mile to the northeast of the lake.

In a large meadow and sink hole is a small entrance to Holmes Cave. Spring and summer snowmelt drain into the entrance of the cave, making it inaccessible. By late summer when it becomes drier is it possible to explore the cave. But it is not an easy cave to spelunk. At the entrance is a dropoff that requires abseils and special climbing equipment to enter the cave safely.

The cave was discovered in 1898 by Edwin B. Holmes, John H. Holland and Neil Matheson, but it was not explored until 1905. It consists of an extensive underground labyrinth of about 0.8 miles and has three chambers: the Wilson, Neda and Holland.

LOST LAKE TRAIL 🚴 🚶 🐎

Length: 1.3 miles, one way.
Elevation change: Trailhead at 9,070 feet (403-foot gain).
Trailhead: A pullout on state highway 26/287 marks the trailhead. This is 3.2 miles west of Togwotee Pass, or 5.8 miles east of Togwotee Lodge.

GREAT HORNED OWL.

This short hike follows an old two-track to a small subalpine lake near the Continental Divide. This site originally was used by the road crew during construction of the Togwotee Pass road to the South Entrance of Yellowstone during the 1910s to 1921. This was one of the crew's base camps, called Road Camp Draw. Up the nearby drainage is a series of springs that served as their source of fresh water.

For the most part, this trail leads through a coniferous forest of subalpine fir and limber pine, and climbs about 400 feet to the small lake.

BROOKS LAKE TRAIL 🚲 ⛷ 🐎

Length: 4.4 miles, one way.
Elevation change: Trailhead at 9,540 feet (374-foot loss).
Trailhead: Located at Wind River Lake picnic area. This small turnout is 0.6 miles southeast of Togwotee Pass, or 6.8 miles west of the entrance to Brooks Lake road.

Brooks Lake Trail is a traditional all-day winter ski trip to an isolated backcountry lodge. But this easygoing trail is ideal for hiking or mountain biking as well. It follows an old road downhill to Brooks Lake, nestled against the Continental Divide.

The trail begins just off the Continental Divide at Togwotee

Pass. The trailhead is marked by a small picnic area. During winter, the road is widened by snowplow, leaving just enough room for a couple of vehicles. From the trailhead, the old road skirts the edge of Sublette Peak (10,537 feet). About 3 miles in, the trail crosses over Barbers Point. The wind blows

SKIING INTO BROOKS LAKE LODGE. APPROACHING BARBERS POINT.

fiercely through this constriction, but the point provides wonderful views of the surrounding countryside. The first views of Pinnacle Buttes, to the northeast, are picturesque.

At Brooks Lake is a campground, from which a number of day hikes or extended hikes originate. Set back from the lake is Brooks Lake Lodge. It was built in 1922, along with the South Entrance road to Yellowstone, and its purpose was to serve as a wayside lodge or dude ranch for visitors traveling to or from Yellowstone. In the late 1980s it was restored and accepts guests during season. Lunch is available for cross-country skiers or snowmobilers. This trip also is a popular overnight stop (reservations required) in a cozy and comfortable lodge.

BIGHORN SHEEP.

From Brooks Lake, it is possible to return to the trailhead via the same route. Another possibility, especially on cross-country skis during winter or mountain bikes during summer, is to return to state highway 26/287 along the Brooks Lake Road. This 5-mile road is not plowed during winter and is open to skiers or snowmobilers only. To return to the trailhead, however, a car shuttle or other transportation is required for the 6.8 mile stretch of highway.

Hiking Signal Mountain

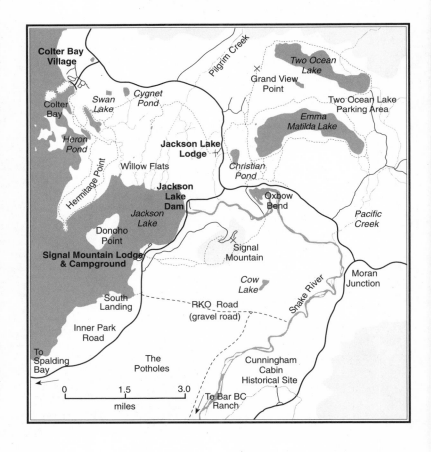

SIGNAL MOUNTAIN

Signal Mountain is the beacon of Grand Teton National Park. It is somewhat of a geologic anomaly in that it rises from the valley floor like a ship on an ocean.

In August of 1890 Robert Ray Hamilton, relative of Alexander Hamilton, disappeared and the sparse community in the valley immediately began a search for him. At first there were rumors of foul play, since his partner, John Sargent, relative of the artist, was suspected of doing him in. The searchers plan was simple. Whoever discovered Hamilton would climb to the top of the nearby knoll and light a signal fire to notify others of the discovery. Days later his body was discovered in what appeared to be an accidental drowning while crossing the river on horseback. And a fire was lit. As a result the knoll became known as Signal Mountain, and the name remains today.

THE TETON RANGE.

From the summit of Signal Mountain it is possible to scan the unusual and varied landscape around this point. The flat glacial outwash plain created during the ice age is visible to the east and south. The deep blue waters of Jackson Lake appear in the foreground to the west with the Teton Range forming the horizon. The Snake River meanders along the base of Signal Mountain to the north, and the Teton Wilderness and Yellowstone National Park continue as far as the eye can see.

The surrounding territory also is the home for herds or congregations of wildlife. In spring cow elk calve in the meadow/forest edge at the base of the mountain and seek protection of the lodgepole forest for the remaining summer. Bison herds, too, can occasionally be seen in the area called the potholes. By looking carefully from the summit of Signal Mountain onto the flat outwash plain it is possible to see the peppered pock marks of thousands of Uinta ground squirrel burrows. Mountain lions also prowl the mountain while bald eagles nest along the river at its base.

MOUNTAIN LION.

All of this and more, including hikes to pioneer cabins and bicycle trips along river terraces is available for explorers to this region of Jackson Hole.

SIGNAL MOUNTAIN TRAIL

Length from Signal Mountain Lodge to:

Moose Pond	0.5 miles, one way.
Signal Mountain Summit	3.0 miles, one way.
Cattlemen's Bridge	5.0 miles, one way.

Elevation change: Trailhead at 6,820 (773-foot gain).
Trailhead: Signal Mountain trailhead and parking is conveniently located—for those staying at Signal Mountain Lodge—at the campground entrance.

This 3-mile trail to the summit of Signal Mountain begins in the parking area at the entrance to the Signal Mountain campground. Walk down the "boat launch" road about 200 yards; a well-marked trail heads east into the lodgepole pines and cuts across the highway, up a steep embankment. The trail continues climbing through lodgepole pines and crosses the Signal Mountain road about two-tenths of a mile from the highway. After crossing the road, continue east past Moose Pond,

often covered with large, yellow, baseball-size pond lilies in late June and early July. The edge of this pond is heavily vegetated and, given time, eventually will fill in and become a low, wet area or a meadow.

Just after Moose Ponds, the trail splits at a junction. The north fork follows the Ridge Trail, and the

FROM SIGNAL MOUNTAIN TRAIL.

south fork follows the Lake Trail past several ponds and Keith Lake. The trails merge again after about a mile. From there, the trails head east for about two-tenths of a mile to a third junction, marked by an old sign.

At this junction, a faint trail heads south and east. This trail contours east, then north below the cliffs of Huckleberry Ridge Tuff and leads to Cattlemen's Bridge for another 3.5 miles. The trail is not

JACKSON HOLE FROM PHOTOGRAPHER W.H. JACKSON'S CAMERA IN 1878.

maintained and downfall is a problem, but old red metal tree markers tag the way. The bridge was built to herd cattle to summer grazing pastures across the Snake River. The other trail from this junction heads north and ascends a gully and switchbacks 1.5 miles up signal Mountain to Jackson Lake Overlook, on the Signal Mountain Road.

Another little-known and less-used trail descends from the summit of Signal Mountain (7,593 feet) on the north side and emerges at Jackson Lake Dam. The trail begins from the last switchback of the Signal Mountain Road. The trail is paved for the first 100 feet to a log bench and a vantage point for Oxbow Bend. From here, the trail begins a steep descent on an unmaintained trail littered with downfall. The trail works its way through Huckleberry Ridge Tuff cliffs and follows a ridge down to the Snake River, where it joins the fishermen's river access to Jackson Lake Dam. This trail is not highly recommended because it is steep, not maintained, and faint in many locations, resembling a game trail. But it does enter prime wildlife country that harbors elk and moose.

SOUTH LANDING TRAIL

Length: 0.5 miles, one way.
Elevation change: Trailhead at 6,890 feet (113-foot loss).
Trailhead: Located 3 miles south of Jackson Lake Dam on the Inner Park Road, or just a quarter mile south of the turnoff to Signal Mountain summit. The parking area is on the west side of the road, directly across from the start of the RKO road.

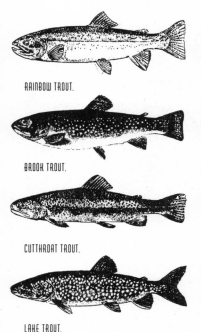

RAINBOW TROUT.

BROOK TROUT.

CUTTHROAT TROUT.

LAKE TROUT.

This short hike provides access to the shore of Jackson Lake and a small secluded cove. The trail is a favorite, especially for locals who hike it to fish, swim, sunbathe or ponder on the lakeshore.

The trailhead is unusual in that it is next to a large abandoned sewage settling pond. On some moist, windy days, the aroma from the source can be overwhelming. Even though this sewage-treatment pond was abandoned long ago, the National Park Service has made no attempt to reclaim this area for health or environmental reasons.

The trail passes the northern edge of the sewage ponds, then begins its descent through lodgepole pines to the shore of Jackson Lake. In this area, the shore is very stony, making it extremely difficult to walk along the shore.

From the cove, the island seen in the distance is Elk Island. It is possible to see Donoho Point, really an island as well, by walking a short distance north along the shore to a point of land. Between Donoho Point and Elk Island is Hermitage Point (see Hermitage Point Trail for description), and a tiny dot of an isle called Marie Island. Farther north along the shore is Signal Mountain campground.

The next bay to the south is Spalding Bay, a popular boating and fishing access.

RKO ROAD

Length from RKO Road/Signal Mountain junction to:

Snake River access spur road junction	2.1 miles, one way.
Snake River access	3.6 miles, one way.
Snake River overlook	7.4 miles, one way.
Steep incline	9.6 miles, one way.
Bar BC Ranch	13.7 miles, one way.
Cottonwood Creek road junction	15.5 miles, one way.
Return via Inner Park Road	28.3 mile loop.

Elevation change: Trailhead at 6,890 feet (237-foot loss at the southern end of RKO Road).
Trailhead: Located 3 miles south of Jackson Lake Dam on the Inner Park Road, or just a quarter mile south of the turnoff to Signal Mountain summit. The dirt road begins on the east side of the paved road, directly across from the start of the South Landing trailhead.

THE SNAKE RIVER FROM RKO ROAD.

The RKO Road is a little-known, but wonderful, hidden road down the center of Jackson Hole. This rough four-wheel drive gravel road accesses and follows the Snake River on a bench overlooking the river bottom lands. From this road are incredible views of the Tetons and one of the few areas where antelope, moose, mule deer, elk and bison can be viewed in one location.

This long road can be hiked and can be made as short or as long as possible by driving any portion of the road, parking and starting from a chosen point. The road is extremely rough, with protruding cobbles in the two-track lane. At about the midway point, an extremely steep river bench intersects the road. The incline is covered with loose gravel and, for traffic heading north, it is nearly impossible to ascend, even for most four-wheel drive vehicles. Thus, it is best to start from the north and travel south, down the gravel incline.

TIGER SALAMANDER.

Even though this is a four-wheel drive road, it is an even better mountain bike trail, especially in spring and early summer, when wildflowers are emerging and blooming. On a mountain bike, front shocks may be a necessity, as the vibration of the cobble road can be overwhelming.

The RKO road begins just south of the Signal Mountain junction, and is a small, nondescript dirt road heading east. This northern section of the road is relatively flat until it junctions with a spur road that accesses the Snake River. The triangular junction is at the edge of a river bench.

The spur road descends and continues east to a spruce-lined bank of the river. This section of road was "improved" and used by the RKO movie studio during its filming of *The Big Sky* (1952) and *Far Horizons* (1955), hence the name of the road. The site also is a popular fishing and raft-launching spot.

At the spur road junction, the RKO road begins its southern route along the Snake River and through postglacial outwash plain. The Pinedale Glaciation—the last of the three major glacial periods ended about 9,000 years ago—created this area. The timbered ridge to the southwest is Burned Ridge, the terminal moraine of Jackson Lake Glacier, which once occupied roughly the area of Jackson Lake. As the climate warmed and the glacier began to retreat, chunks of glacial ice were buried under silt, sand and cobbles. Later, the buried ice melted, leaving depressions. Some filled with water, creating kettle lakes. Between Burned Ridge and the road is a region of these depressions called The Potholes. During summer, this is a popular area for the bison herd.

For the most part, this road follows the edge of a high river bench and provides some incredible views of the river bottom. One of the best views is achieved near the southern tip of Burned Ridge, where the road is closet to the river at a steep embankment. To the east, along a curve in the river, is Deadman's Bar, where four German prospectors searched for gold during the summer of 1886. One man killed his three partners, pitched the bodies over an embankment and covered them with rocks. A few weeks later, fishermen discovered the decomposing bodies. The surviving prospector was found working at a nearby ranch and was tried but acquitted on the grounds of self-defense and circumstantial evidence.

Southeast across the river from the vantage point is the Snake River Overlook, where it is possible to spy viewers on the stone and concrete overlook.

Just beyond the Snake River overlook, the road junctions with an old road that once led west to Timbered Island and Jenny Lake. The road was reclaimed in the mid-1980s, but a faint outline still is visible through the sagebrush. At this point, the road reaches the steep, gravelly descent of the river bench and again parallels the river along another open sagebrush bench all the way to the Bar BC Ranch (see Bar BC Ranch Trail for description).

THE RKO ROAD ALONG THE SNAKE RIVER BENCH.

From the ranch—one of the oldest dude ranches in the valley and now in ruins—the road heads west up another river bench and across the sagebrush flat, where it meets with the Inner Park Road near Cottonwood Creek bridge.

The RKO Road is 15.5 miles long, and for a mountain-bike loop, if a car shuttle has not been arranged, add another 12.8 miles of paved road back to the beginning.

SPALDING BAY SHORELINE

Length: Open-ended shoreline.
Elevation change: Trailhead at 6,772 feet. (no perceptual elevation change).
Trailhead: The lakeshore is accessed via the Spalding Bay road. This 2.1 mile gravel road begins just off the north Jenny Lake junction.

Spalding Bay is not much of a trail but provides access to the shore of Jackson Lake and the rocky, cobble lakeshore that can be hiked in either direction, north or south.

The Spalding Bay road heads north from the north Jenny Lake junction, through Douglas fir and lodgepole pine, to the shore of the lake. This road and shore is primarily a small-boat launch site. But there is a picnic area and it is possible to walk any distance along the shoreline. This also is a great fishing access.

RIVER OTTER.

Evident along the road and lakeshore is burned forest from the 1981 Mystic Isle fire.

CUNNINGHAM CABIN TRAIL

Length: 0.3 mile loop.
Elevation change: Trailhead at 6,760 feet (no perceptual elevation change).
Trailhead: The parking area is at the end of the Cunningham Cabin road. This is a short 0.4 mile paved road, and the turnoff for this is 5.4 miles south of Buffalo River bridge, or 24.7 miles north of Jackson.

This short hike among the ruins of an old homestead is a leisurely stroll that can easily be accomplished before or after another hike.

The remains, primarily consisting of foundation stones and depressions, are the site of J. Pierce Cunningham's Bar Fly U Ranch. Cunningham and his wife, Margaret, homesteaded in Jackson Hole in 1890. They also had a homestead in the southern valley on Flat Creek, where the climate was somewhat milder during winter.

This ranch was used primarily for hay production, as the moist grassy meadows produced abundant hay by late July. The grass usually was cut by a horse-drawn cutter, then was allowed to dry and cure. A horse-drawn raker then would rake it into windrows. The hay would be thrown by hand onto a stacker— a large loom-like device—and, with the aid of horses, would be lifted via pulleys and loosely stacked as winter feed for live-stock.

The small cabin with a pole and sod roof is a reconstruction of an original cabin built on the site. This replica was built by the Jackson Hole Preserve in the 1950s. It was believed that the original structure was a barn and tack room.

An interesting event, known as the "Cunningham Cabin Affair" occurred here in the winter of 1893. Two men, Spenser and Burnett, purchased hay from Pierce Cunningham, who allowed them

CUNNINGHAM CABIN.

to use his homestead. It turned out that the two men were horse thieves who decided to winter and 'hole up' in the valley with their contraband. By early spring, two other men snowshoed over Teton Pass and, saying they were lawmen from Montana— it was never determined if they were official—collected a seven-man posse and trudged up to the homestead. At dawn, they surrounded the cabin and called Spenser and Burnett out. They came out shooting, but were shot down. The posse wrapped the men's bodies in blankets and buried them in shallow graves. They vowed secrecy, but the story was revealed years later.

HIKING JENNY LAKE

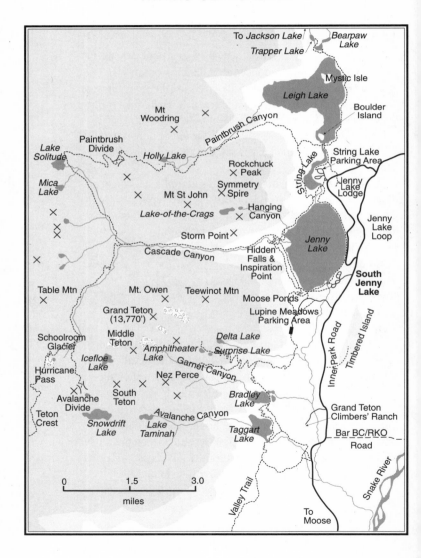

JENNY LAKE

When the words Jackson Hole or Grand Teton are mentioned the name Jenny Lake is conjured shortly after. Jenny Lake is synonymous with Jackson Hole, and rightly so. It is the crossroads for all major hikes in the Teton Range. Hikes including, Jenny, String or Leigh lakes, Cascade Canyon, Hidden Falls, Inspiration Point, Lake Solitude, Paintbrush Divide, Hurricane Pass, Schoolroom Glacier, Alaska Basin, Surprise and Amphitheater Lakes, Hanging, Avalanche or Garnet canyons, and the Teton Crest and Valley trails are just a few originating from here.

It also is the point of departure for mountaineers and climbers of the major peaks, including the Grand, Middle and South Teton, Mount Teewinot and other climbing destinations that top the Teton Range.

THE GRAND TETON AND MOUNT TEEWINOT DOMINATE THE JENNY LAKE AREA.

But beyond the rigors of climbing and hiking is the beauty and tranquility of the mountains and the glacial lakes at their feet. Trails or boats lead from the congested summertime parking area to isolated spots along tumultuous streams, sandy beaches or scenic summits.

It was here during the summer of 1872 that the southern unit of the Hayden Survey, lead by Stevenson, journeyed into Jackson Hole. They were guided by a white trapper, Richard "Beaver Dick" Leigh, and his Shoshoni Indian wife, Jenny. The surveyors charted, mapped, climbed the peaks, photographed the landscape and left their names on landmarks for posterity. Jenny and Leigh lakes were named in honor of their guides. Bradley and Taggart lakes in honor of the expeditions geologists. Mount Moran was named in honor of landscape artist Thomas Moran, even though he never stepped into Jackson Hole. Mount Hayden—the grandest peak of all—was named after the expedition's leader, but the name was later changed to Grand Teton.

OREGON GRAPE.

STRING & LEIGH LAKES TRAIL

Length from String Lake parking area to:

Leigh Lake outlet	0.9 miles, one way.
Leigh Lake spur trail	1.0 mile, one way.
String Lake Trail junction	1.5 miles, one way.
Jenny Lake Trail junction	2.9 miles, one way.
String Lake Trail loop	3.5 mile loop.

Elevation change: Trailhead at 6,873 feet (15-foot gain to Leigh Lake, but a 267-foot gain at String Lake Trail junction).
Trailhead: The trail begins at the north end of the String Lake parking area. The String Lake parking and picnic area is located along Jenny Lake loop road.

SILVERY LUPINE.

String and Leigh lakes trail is a good afternoon hike in July and August, especially when the valley lakes have warmed enough for a good swim. This trail also parallels one of the best canoe trips in Grand Teton.

Most canoers put in at String Lake and canoe up the mile long lake to a short tenth of a mile portage to Leigh Lake. Where another lake beckons to be explored. There are even a number of campsites along the shore of Leigh Lake for overnight adventurers.

The trailhead begins at the north end of the String Lake parking area. From there the leisurely path follows the shoreline of String Lake. The shore is, however, lined with lodgepole pines, mountain alder and fool's huckleberry shrubs.

After about a mile, the trail junctions. The east trail leads to Leigh Lake. The north trail continues around String Lake.

The short spur trail to Leigh lake is highly rewarding. It also is the canoe portage. The trail leads to an embankment and a steep, eroded drop to the lakeshore. From this point, it is easy to see Boulder Island, just a stone's throw from the shore. Even though the island is close by for a swim, it is far enough for hypothermia to develop in the cold glacier-fed water. In the past, several swimmers have drowned while attempting to swim there and back from the shore.

To the north, in the distance, is another island which burned in a 1981 lightning strike fire. The fire spread across the lake from Mystic Isle and traveled across the mainland before it was controlled by firefighting efforts. Today, the island is covered with the skeletons of a once-dense forest.

MOUNT MORAN AND BOULDER ISLAND.

From Leigh Lake portage, the trail continues along the east shore of Leigh Lake to several sandy beaches and Bearpaw Lake (see Bearpaw Lake Trail for description).

At Leigh Lake junction and lake outlet, the trail crosses the stream via a foot bridge, then around several large glacial erratics to one of the best huckleberry patches in Jackson Hole. The trail then begins a climb to String Lake/Paintbrush Canyon Trail junction. There the north trail heads into Paintbrush Canyon (see Paintbrush Canyon Trail for description) and the south trail continues around String Lake, along the base of Rockchuck Peak and Mount St. John, overlooking String Lake.

This section of the trail passes through several interesting features. One is an escarpment created by the Teton Fault. This is one of the few visible fault lines, but it is best viewed from a distance, especially from the Jenny Lake Lodge area.

The Teton Fault runs along the base of the Teton Range. On average, the Teton Range rises about one foot every 100 years. Jackson Hole has not had a major earthquake in recorded history, though it is long overdue. Stresses in the earth are continuing to accumulate, and when they are released, expect a few new fault lines in this area.

The slope also shows the effect of avalanches. The trail passes through several old and new avalanche chutes. During winter, the

STRING LAKE WITH TEEWINOT MOUNTAIN AND THE GRAND TETON.

slope is too steep to hold the weight of heavy snow accumulation, and gravity takes over. When snow does slide, it sheers off trees, carries boulders and leaves rubble at the base of the mountain on the shore of String Lake. By summer, the snow has melted, leaving a twisted mass of tree trunks and dirt at the bottom, and what appears to be a groomed ski slope above.

After passing through an avalanche chute, the trail begins descending to the lake and enters the lodgepole forest again, then junctions with the Jenny Lake Trail (see Jenny Lake Trail for description). From there, it follows the fast-moving stream between String and Jenny lakes. This short stretch of water is popular for fishing, but more for its scenery than good fishing.

The trail crosses the outlet of String Lake by way of a footbridge and emerges at the beginning of the String Lake parking and picnic area.

PAINTBRUSH CANYON TRAIL
Length from String Lake parking area to:
Leigh Lake outlet	0.9 miles, one way.
String Lake Trail junction	1.5 miles, one way.

Holly Lake	6.2 miles, one way.
Mount Woodring spur trail	7.2 miles, one way.
Paintbrush Divide	7.9 miles, one way.
Lake Solitude	10.4 miles, one way.
Jenny Lake parking area	19.2 miles, one way.
String Lake parking area (return)	22.5 mile loop.

Elevation change: Trailhead at 6,873 feet (3,807-foot gain to Paintbrush Divide).

Trailhead: The trail begins at the north end of the String Lake parking area. The String Lake parking and picnic area is located along the Jenny Lake loop road.

Paintbrush Canyon remains the classic quintessential trail of Jackson Hole. The trail leads along tranquil valley lakes, through lodgepole forests, into a glaciated canyon, to subalpine lakes and a mountain pass topped with subalpine wildflowers.

The Paintbrush Canyon Trail starts at the end of the String Lake parking and picnic area. From here, it leads to the outlet of Leigh Lake, where it turns west at a junction and crosses the front of String Lake via a footbridge.

On the other side of the bridge and just beyond several large glacial erratics is one of the best huckleberry patches in Jackson Hole. This small sparse shrub covers the lodgepole forest floor. The small blueberry-like berries are borne individually, not clustered. But this is one of the largest and best-producing patches when the berries begin to ripen by the end of the first or second week of August.

FOOL'S HUCKLEBERRY.

Black bears also relish huckleberries and, with their keen sense of smell, are able to locate them from a mile away. It is not unusual to find a black bear in this huckleberry patch, stripping away the berries and occasional leaves with its very prehensile tongue and lips.

Just beyond the huckleberry patch, the trail begins its climb and, after passing a small pond, comes to a junction. The String Lake Trail (see String Lake Trail for description)

BIG HUCKLEBERRY.

heads south along the base of the mountain, and overlooks String Lake. The north trail heads into Paintbrush Canyon and is a relatively gradual climb until it merges with the creek. From this area is a wonderful view of Leigh Lake and Mystic Isle. The trail then begins a series of switchbacks, emerging at a meadow with two small lakes. The largest is Holly Lake. During summer, the wildflower display here is incredible. Yellow subalpine buttercups, white marsh marigolds, pink mountain heather and purple mountain gentian dot the slopes.

Camping is available in the Holly Lake area, but a backcountry camping permit is required—though it may be difficult to come by, as this is a highly popular camp spot.

A one-mile spur trail and a scramble leads northwest from Holly Lake, then follows a ridge to the summit of Mount Woodring (11,590 feet). This is a popular and easy mountain-climbing summit to reach. Mount Woodring is named

VIEW OF THE GRAND FROM MOUNT WOODRING.

after Samuel Woodring, Grand Teton National Park's first superintendent, who was forced to flee the valley by local residents when they discovered his child-molesting activities.

Mount Woodring rises directly north of Holly Lake and, from the summit it offers an especially good view of Thor Peak and Mount Moran to the north, and to the east down Paintbrush Canyon and the Grand to the south.

From Holly Lake, the trail continues its uphill grind via a few more switchbacks to Paintbrush Divide. The north side of the divide, just before the pass, usually is covered in snow until mid-July, and even after that are patches of ice in the more protected crannies. Be extremely cautious in crossing these snow patches, and wear safety gear where necessary.

On the windswept divide, snuggled in cracks between rocks, are small, mat-forming blue alpine forget-me-not and pink moss campion.

MOSS CAMPION.

From the divide the trail descends into the North Fork of Cascade Canyon (see Lake Solitude and the North Fork of Cascade Canyon Trail for description). Due west is a view of Lake Solitude. The trail continues down into Cascade Canyon and returns to Jenny or String lakes via this route.

BEARPAW LAKE TRAIL

Length from String Lake parking area to:

Leigh Lake outlet	0.9 miles, one way.
Leigh Lake	1.0 mile, one way.
Sandy beach	2.0 miles, one way.
Leigh Lake patrol cabin	3.6 miles, one way.
Bearpaw Lake	3.9 miles, one way.
Trapper Lake	4.2 miles, one way.
Bearpaw Bay	5.0 miles, one way.

Elevation change: Trailhead at 6,873 feet (4-foot gain to Leigh Lake, but a 25-foot loss to Bearpaw Lake).

Trailhead: The trail begins at the north end of the String Lake parking area. The String Lake parking and picnic area is located along the Jenny Lake loop road.

WYOMING PAINTBRUSH.

Bearpaw Lake Trail is a pleasant stroll along a series of lakes at the foot of the Tetons. There is little elevation change as the trail begins at String Lake, ambles past Leigh Lake and emerges at Bearpaw Lake. From there, the trail continues on to Trapper Lake and ends on the shore of Jackson Lake at Bearpaw Bay.

For the first mile, this trail uses the String lake Trail (see String & Leigh Lakes Trail for description). At Leigh Lake, it continues along the east shore of the lake. The views

VIEW OF MOUNT MORAN FROM LEIGH LAKE.

of Mount Moran rising from the other side of the lake are wonderful. About halfway along the lake shore is a small sandy beach. On warm summer days, this is an ideal place to take a dip—albeit a cold one—in the lake, and sunbathe on the beach.

Just beyond the beach is a small island called Mystic Isle. A lightning-caused forest fire started here in 1981 and burned the lush vegetation on the island. The fire also jumped across the water and burned the mainland from the shore east to Jackson Lake. Burned trees are still evident along the northern portion of Leigh Lake.

On the north shore is a patrol cabin that usually is occupied during summer. From Leigh Lake, it is a short distance to Bearpaw Lake, a small lodgepole and subalpine tree-lined lake. And just beyond Bearpaw Lake is Trapper Lake, an even smaller lake at the base of Mount Moran.

JENNY LAKE AND CASCADE CANYON FROM THE AIR.

Bearpaw Bay on Jackson Lake is accessed either by following the outlet of Bearpaw Lake or bushwhacking though the woods in a northeasterly direction. Before the bay, however, hikers must circumvent a marshy, mud flat.

JENNY LAKE TRAIL

Length: 6.5 mile loop.

Elevation change: Trailhead at 6,790 feet (no perceptual elevation change).

Trailhead: Several access points are available: 1) The most popular starting point is the Jenny Lake boat dock; 2) or starting halfway around the lake at String Lake bridge.

Jenny Lake was named after the Indian wife of trapper guide Richard "Beaver Dick" Leigh, who guided members of Stevenson's Snake River division of the 1872 Hayden Expedition. To honor their guide, they named the lake after his Shoshone wife and named the other large lake a mile and a half north, Leigh Lake, for "Beaver Dick."

The trail around the lake is easygoing and starts at either

the Jenny Lake or String Lake parking area. During summer, it is most enjoyable in morning or evening, when it is cooler and fewer people are around. The trail's drawback during summer is that it parallels, or in some cases adjoins, the road on the east side of the lake.

For winter skiing, access to Jenny Lake adds additional mileage. The road is usually plowed from the south to the Bradley-Taggart parking area on Cottonwood Creek. A cross-country ski trail generally follows Cottonwood Creek from the parking area north to Jenny Lake. Or, some ski the barren, windswept, exposed, snow covered road to the lake. Either route adds 4 miles one way en route to the lake, with a 6.5 mile trip around its circumference.

CROSSING JENNY BY BOAT.

During summer, the trail provides an exciting excursion around the shore of the lake. Black bears often will have day beds next to the trail, and hundreds of hikers will pass by without realizing that a sleeping bear is nearby. Wildflowers also abound along the trail. On the east shore are yellow arrowleaf balsamroots, white Engelmann asters and the locally rare Brown's peony. Red raspberries, white-flowered thimbleberries and purple monkshood find suitable habitat on the moist west shore at the base of the mountains.

Jenny Lake is a young lake, geologically speaking. It was formed during the last and most recent glacial period, the Pinedale Glaciation. The last of the great glaciers ended about 9,000 years ago. Before that, however, they created most of the landscape visible from the lake. Cascade Canyon originally was cut by streams that formed it into a V-shape. When glaciers later flowed down the canyon, they sculpted and broadened the canyon into a wide U-shape. The sharp peaks surrounding Cascade Canyon and Jenny Lake, including the Grand Teton, Teewinot Mountain, Storm Point and Mount St. John, were cut into their distinct "matterhorn" shapes by the frozen rivers.

BROWN'S PEONY.

As it receded up Cascade Canyon the last of the great glaciers deposited glacial rock at its toe, or terminus. The eastern shore of Jenny Lake was formed by the terminal moraine of this glacier, and the north and south shores by lateral moraines. They are composed of unconsolidated glacial till, which comprises everything from small particles of silt and sand to pebbles, cobbles and large boulders, called glacial erratics.

As the weather warmed and the glacier receded, the melting ice filled the basin, forming Jenny Lake. As the climate warmed, the glacier receded all the way up Cascade Canyon.

Today, only a remnant of that ancient glacier exists at the head of the South Fork of Cascade Canyon in the form of a little chunk of flowing ice called Schoolroom Glacier.

In 1933, unusual cyclonic, windsheering winds hit the Jenny Lake campground on the east shore of the lake, slashing a half-mile-

JENNY LAKE BOAT DOCK.

wide swath. Trees were uprooted, toppling like toothpicks and being left aligned facing one direction. Then, in November of 1973, similar winds struck again, leveling the trees in the campground and the southern end of the lake. This last strike still is visible from the shore.

The Jenny Lake hike also accesses one of the most popular hikes in Grand Teton National Park, the trail to Cascade Canyon (see Cascade Canyon for description), including Hidden Falls, Inspiration Point and beyond to lake Solitude (see respective trails for descriptions). The trail also provides access to Moose Ponds (see Moose Ponds Trail for description), the String Lake Trail (see String Lake Trail for description) and the climbers route to Hanging Canyon Trail (see Hanging Canyon Trail for description) and Lake-of-the-Crags.

MOOSE PONDS TRAIL 🏊

Length from Jenny Lake parking area to:

Moose Ponds Trail junction	0.6 miles, one way.
Moose Ponds	0.9 miles, one way.

Elevation change: Trailhead at 6,790 feet (no perceptual elevation change).

Trailhead: Located at the southern shore of Jenny Lake at the developed parking area.

This short trail is an ideal early morning or late evening hike originating from Jenny Lake. It is ideal for locating wildlife including Moose, deer, beaver, muskrat or waterfowl. During midsummer, before the midday crowds arrive, this trail provides a great early morning stroll, but wildlife are usually higher in the mountains at this time of year. The best seasons for increasing the probability of sighting wildlife is early spring or late fall. At those times the ponds are a sanctuary.

The trail begins at the Jenny Lake boat dock and follows the Jenny Lake Trail (see Jenny Lake Trail for description) along the southern shore. At the very southern tip is a trail junction leading to the ponds. This is an old horse trail used by horse ride concessionaires based at Jenny Lake until the early 1990s. From the junction the trail loops through an old picnic ground to the ponds. From there it is possible to loop around the ponds and merge with the Lupine Meadows parking area. Otherwise the trail rejoins the Jenny Lake Trail. After that junction is a wonderful overlook of the ponds. This is the best location to get an overview and discover what creatures are there before descending to the ponds and examining them closer.

BUFFLEHEAD.

HIDDEN FALLS & INSPIRATION POINT TRAIL

Length from Jenny Lake parking area and boat dock (or String Lake parking area):

Hidden Falls	2.3 miles, one way.
Inspiration Point	2.8 miles, one way.

Length from Jenny Lake west shore boat dock:

Hidden Falls	0.5 miles, one way.
Inspiration Point	1.0 mile, one way.

Elevation change: Trailhead at 6,785 feet (515-foot gain to Inspiration Point).
Trailhead: Located at the southern shore of Jenny Lake at the developed parking area.

Hidden Falls and Inspiration Point trails are two of the most popular, and on summer days, the most crowded, hikes in Grand Teton National Park. These hikes also serve as the gateway to Cascade Canyon and Lake Solitude.

There are three ways to reach Hidden Falls and Inspiration Point. The first is to hike from Jenny Lake parking area along

the southern shore of Jenny Lake. This trail is a portion of the Jenny Lake Trail (see Jenny Lake Trail for description). It then splits off and follows Cascade Creek to the falls. This route around the lake but only to the junction is about 1.8 miles, plus an additional half mile to the falls.

The second option is to take the shuttle boat (for a fee) from Jenny Lake parking area to the west-shore boat dock. The east-shore boat dock is 300 yards west of the parking area at the outlet of Jenny Lake. Taking the boat shuttle reduces the hiking distance by 1.8 miles. The boats leave or return about every 15 minutes throughout the

HIDDEN FALLS.   day during summer, with the last boat returning at 6 p.m.

The third route involves the northwestern section of Jenny Lake Trail. This route begins at String Lake parking area and follows the shoreline to a junction with Hidden Falls Trail. Like the southern one, this route to the junction is about 1.8 miles.

After arriving at Cascade Creek junction, or the west-shore boat dock from any direction, the trail then follows Cascade Creek for nearly a half mile to the falls. Along the way, the trail passes steep narrow gorges where the tumultuous waters of Cascade Creek churn over the rocky impediments. The trail in this section is a steep, deeply rutted one with stair-step-like rocks. Above the point, the creek is a bit calmer and the trail crosses the creek via a footbridge. The water beside the bridge is crystal clear and, on hot summer days, is a natural swimming hole. But the water is icy cold, in the mid-40°F range.

On the other side of the footbridge is an area of exposed, highly polished bedrock. By looking closely it is possible to see scratches and grooves created 9,000 to 12,000 years ago, when the last of the Pinedale glaciers were actively flowing down Cascade Canyon. Beyond the glacially polished rock, the trail continues through Engelmann spruce, Douglas fir and lodge-pole pine forest until the forest canopy opens to a large rock talus slope. This jumble of large boulders is the home of pikas, and their call, a sharp *"pee,"* is very distinctive. They are difficult to spot, as their brownish coats are the same colors as the boulders on which they sit. But by watching the rocks carefully and detecting any movement, it is possible to spot the small mammals. Even though pikas resemble rabbits and hares, they belong to a separate family. Pikas have short, broad rounded ears and no visible tails. During most of the summer, they harvest grasses, sedges and raspberry leaves. They spread these "haystacks" out to dry, then store them in crevices under the boulders of the talus slope for winter forage.

Just after the talus slope and before another footbridge across Cascade Creek is a spur trail leading to Hidden Falls. It is a short trail and the falls are truly hidden up to the base. Before reaching the vantage point on a hot summer day, notice the temperature change.

Hidden Falls is not actually a true falls at all, but a cascade. A cascade is a series of small waterfalls tumbling over steep rocks, as opposed to steep, free-falling water from a height.

JENNY LAKE FROM
INSPIRATION POINT.

To reach Inspiration Point, continue up the trail, crossing the footbridge and moving along the steep trail cut into bedrock. This is the first of several cliffside switchbacks blasted out of bedrock by the Park Service during the 1960s through the 1980s. Each successive cliffside exposure provides an ever-better view of Jenny Lake until Inspiration Point is reached.

Between the last two cliffside exposures, the trail leads into the forest, where the trail is deeply entrenched. This trail cut exposes ash from the Mount Mazama—Crater Lake, Oregon—eruption that occurred nearly 6,800 years ago. At that time, nearly 25 cubic miles of ash and volcanic debris were ejected from the volcano. The ash spread eastward with prevailing winds and coated most of the Pacific Northwest. Most of the ash has eroded, but small protected pockets remain. Here along the trail is an isolated pocket of Mount Mazama ash that is nearly a foot and a half thick.

At Inspiration Point is a wonderful view of Jenny Lake, Jackson Hole and, on the horizon, the Gros Ventre Mountains. From this 7,200-foot vantage, it is possible to reconstruct the formation of Jenny Lake by the receding glaciers.

Scurrying among the rocks at Inspiration Point are chipmunk-like golden-mantled ground squirrels. They are much larger than chipmunks and lack that animal's common eyestripe. But they have adapted the chipmunk behavior of begging tidbits from hikers and are even bold enough to enter backpacks and climb pant legs for their treats.

GOLDEN-MANTLED
GROUND SQUIRREL.

The trail continues beyond Inspiration Point up Cascade Canyon (see Cascade Canyon Trail for description) to Cascade Canyon fork, which then leads either north to Lake Solitude or south to Schoolroom Glacier.

CASCADE CANYON TRAIL

Length from Jenny Lake parking area & boat dock (or String Lake parking area) to:

Hidden Falls	2.3 miles, one way.
Inspiration Point	2.8 miles, one way.
Cascade Canyon fork	6.4 miles, one way.

Length from Jenny Lake west shore boat dock to:

Hidden Falls	0.5 miles, one way.

Inspiration Point   1.0 miles, one way.
Cascade Canyon fork   4.6 miles, one way.
Elevation change: Trailhead at 6,785 feet (1,055-foot gain).
Trailhead: Located at the southern shore of Jenny Lake at the developed parking area. Or an alternative route from String Lake picnic area.

Cascade Canyon Trail is one way to get into the mountains and experience their immenseness. This trail is by far the most popular and crowded of the canyon trails, but it is the crossroads for hiking and climbing. Most of the major trails or destinations originate or merge here.

There are three routes available to reach the start of Cascade Canyon. Two of the routes use the Hidden Falls and Inspiration Point Trail (see Hidden Falls & Inspiration Point Trail for description), using either the boat shuttle (for a fee) across

GROUSE WHORTLEBERRY, A SMALL BROOM-LIKE SHRUB, BEARING HUCKLEBERRY FRUIT.

the lake or by foot along the southern shore. Another route is along the north shore of Jenny Lake. This trailhead begins at the entrance to the String Lake picnic area. It starts with a bridge crossing at the outlet of String Lake and joins the lakeshore all the way to the junction with the Hidden Falls Trail. Shortly

CASCADE CANYON.

before the junction there also is a shortcut horse trail that bypasses Hidden Falls and Inspiration Point, rejoining the Cascade Canyon Trail just above Inspiration Point.

The climb to Inspiration Point is half the gain and from here to the canyon fork it is relatively gradual.

All along the trail are intermittent calm and turbulent stretches of Cascade Creek. In some of the first tranquil stretches of the pond-like creek moose can often be found. Moose usually migrate into the canyon during the summer and it is one of their favorite areas.

In several locations is evidence of rock slides. Some are

FLOWER SPIDER.

PARRY'S PRIMROSE.

ancient, but a few are very recent and the trail crosses several toes of these. They are a reminder that geologic processes are still occurring.

Most of the forest is comprised of old growth Engelmann spruce mixed in with lodgepole pine. Thimbleberry, raspberry and huckleberry—all small shrubs—line the trail. The twisted form and five needle bundles of limber pine also become evident farther up the canyon. At Cascade fork is one of the largest known limber pines.

At the fork is the decision to split in one of two directions. The North Fork leads to Lake Solitude and Paintbrush Divide (see Lake Solitude-North Fork Cascade Canyon Trail for description), or the South Fork leads to Schoolroom Glacier and Hurricane Pass (see Schoolroom Glacier-South Fork Cascade Canyon Trail for description).

LAKE SOLITUDE-NORTH FORK CASCADE CANYON TRAIL

Length from Jenny Lake parking area & boat dock (or String Lake parking area):

Hidden Falls	2.3 miles, one way.
Inspiration Point	2.8 miles, one way.
Cascade Canyon fork	6.4 miles, one way.
Lake Solitude	8.8 miles, one way.
Paintbrush Divide	11.3 miles, one way.

Length from Jenny Lake west shore boat dock:

Hidden Falls	0.5 miles, one way.
Inspiration Point	1.0 miles, one way.
Cascade Canyon fork	4.6 miles, one way.
Lake Solitude	7.0 miles, one way.
Paintbrush Divide	9.5 miles, one way.

Elevation change: Trailhead at 6,785 feet (2,250-foot gain to Lake Solitude 3,895-foot gain to Paintbrush Divide).

Trailhead: Located on the southern shore of Jenny Lake at the developed parking area. Or an alternative route from String Lake picnic area.

The hike to Lake Solitude is the most popular day-long hike in Grand Teton National Park. It is a relatively gentle, easy-going hike that leads to a small tarn lake situated in the cirque or the head of the North Fork of Cascade Canyon.

To reach this section of Cascade Canyon Trail a series of trails are necessary. The first is Hidden Falls & Inspiration Point (see Hidden Falls & Inspiration Point Trail for description), and the other is Cascade Canyon (see Cascade Canyon Trail for description). These two trails lead to the fork of Cascade Canyon.

From the fork the trail begins a slightly steeper ascent, first through Engelmann spruce and limber pine. The trail soon afterward emerges from the forest and through a jumble of boulders into the upper meadows of the North Fork.

This canyon has a unique glacial history. Scoured walls and a broad U-shape canyon are clues to its past, and this evidence is visible while walking up the North Fork.

Lake Solitude (9,035 feet) is a small, glacial tarn, or lake located in a cirque. The view to the southeast, down the valley, is one of the best and provides a unique aspect of the Grand Teton. Ice usually remains on the lake until mid July, because of its altitude and the shading of the canyon wall.

For most hikers Lake Solitude is the final destination and the return is all down hill. However the trail does continue on and upward via a series of switchbacks over paintbrush Divide (10,680 feet) and then down Paintbrush Canyon (see Paintbrush Canyon Trail for description) to String Lake. This entire hike can be accomplished as an extremely long day hike of 19.2 miles (plus an additional 3.3 miles to Jenny Lake parking area for a complete roundtrip loop). But most hikers go up Cascade Canyon and cross Paintbrush Divide to camp overnight at Holly Lake (9,410 feet). A backcountry permit is required and acquiring a permit is difficult because of its popularity.

SCHOOLROOM GLACIER-SOUTH FORK CASCADE CANYON TRAIL
Length from Jenny Lake parking area & boat dock (or String Lake parking area) to:

Hidden Falls	2.3 miles, one way.
Inspiration Point	2.8 miles, one way.
Cascade Canyon fork	6.4 miles, one way.
Avalanche Divide Trail junction	10.1 miles, one way.
Avalanche Divide spur trail	11.6 miles, one way.
Schoolroom Glacier	10.8 miles, one way.
Hurricane Pass	11.2 miles, one way.

Length from Jenny Lake west shore boat dock to:

Hidden Falls	0.5 miles, one way.
Inspiration Point	1.0 miles, one way.
Cascade Canyon fork	4.6 miles, one way.
Avalanche Divide Trail junction	8.3 miles, one way.
Avalanche Divide spur trail	9.8 miles, one way.
Schoolroom Glacier	9.0 miles, one way.
Hurricane Pass	9.4 miles, one way.

Elevation change: Trailhead at 6,785 feet (3,605-foot gain to Hurricane Pass).

Trailhead: Located at the southern shore of Jenny Lake at the developed parking area. Or an alternative route from String Lake picnic area.

The South Fork Cascade Canyon, like the North Fork, is a unique and fascinating trail. It wanders along tumultuous streams, past the base of the three Tetons, to the perfect glacier and up to a pass which provides a view of it all.

The South Fork is approached by utilizing the Inspiration Point Trail (see Hidden Falls and Inspiration Point Trails for description) and the Cascade Canyon Trail (see Cascade Canyon Trail for description). These two trails lead to the fork of Cascade Canyon and the beginning of this trail.

Almost from the start the scenery and natural features are spectacular. Cascade Creek plunges down chutes and cascades for the first mile, and the trail weaves in and around the stream, providing a perspective and up close views.

Soon afterward the trail enters a tranquil meadow, lush with summer wildflowers. Brook saxifrage, alumroot, marsh

ONE-SIDED
WINTERGREEN.

marigolds, mitrewort and Parry's primrose are all found in moist to wet areas along the streams and springs.

From the meadow the trail climbs what appears to be a bench to a higher meadow. At this meadow is a trail junction to Avalanche Divide. This mile and a half spur trail climbs nearly 1,030 feet to the pass. At the pass is a great view of The Wall and of Snowdrift Lake to the south. Most of this area is snowed in until mid to late July. From here is a mountaineer's trail connecting to Avalanche Canyon (see Avalanche Canyon Trail for description), however, it is only a mountaineer's trail and is used to access climbing routes and peaks. The trail is not maintained because of snow, ice and rock conditions. The best and safest route is to return down Cascade Canyon.

SOUTH FORK
CASCADE CANYON.

From Avalanche Divide Trail junction the trail climbs again to another meadow at the bottom of Schoolroom Glacier.

Schoolroom Glacier is a small glacier, less than a quarter square mile in size. It possesses all the features of a classic 'school book' glacier. At the base is a crescent-shaped berm, called a moraine. The sides are referred to as lateral moraines and the toe a terminal moraine. These are formed by flowing ice plucking and carrying rock from the headwall to a point where the ice melts, depositing its load at the moraine.

Behind the moraine is a small lake. The ice is retreating enough that the moraine acts as a natural dam, retaining the melted ice water. Above the lake is glacial ice with its toe in the lake and its head in the cirque or headwall.

Glaciers are basically frozen rivers. These frozen rivers in Grand Teton move between a few feet to tens of feet a year. During winter snow accumulates, sometimes up to 50 feet a year on top of a glacier, and as new snow falls the bottom layers become compressed. With time the bottom layers are so compressed by the overburden that most of the air is squeezed

SCARLET GILIA.

out of the ice. Glacial ice is dense and heavy, and because of gravity, begins to slowly flow like melted plastic.

With warm summer temperatures there is less accumulation, but some near the head of the glacier. At the toe, however, ice can no longer remain in a frozen state and begins to melt. The runoff either fills a lake behind the moraine or forms an outwash plain below.

If the climate remains stable year after year a glacier remains uniform in size and location. But if the climate becomes colder for an extended period the glacier advances farther downhill and retreats with a warmer climate. In this way a glacier becomes a barometer of climatic conditions. Schoolroom Glacier has been studied for this reason. Between the last 100 to 400 years this region experienced a mini ice age and Schoolroom Glacier was active and formed its moraine. Since then Schoolroom Glacier has been retreating. During the 1900s to late 1930s Schoolroom Glacier remained stationary. Beginning in the late 1930s, however, the toe of the glacier was close to the moraine and now has retreated up to the headwall, and if the climate continues warming Schoolroom Glacier will become extinct.

The best location to view the glacier is from Hurricane Pass. From there is an incredible panoramic view of the glacier, South Fork and the backside of the three Tetons—The Grand, Middle and South Teton. *Les Trois Tetons* the french trappers called them.

Hurricane Pass is directly on the forest/national park boundary, and the boundary follows the ridge north and intersects Table Mountain.

From Hurricane Pass the trail steps out of Grand Teton National Park. For most hikers continuing on the Teton Crest Trail (see Teton crest Trail for description), the trail heads south into Alaska Basin. Another trail heading west down into Roaring Creek is a bushwhack trail that does eventually merge with Teton Canyon Trail on the Idaho side. This is not a well-traveled trail and thus is not highly recommended.

TETON CREST TRAIL-NORTH

Length from Jenny Lake parking area & boat dock (or String Lake parking area) to:

Hidden Falls	2.3 miles, one way.
Inspiration Point	2.8 miles, one way.
Cascade Canyon fork	6.4 miles, one way.
Avalanche Divide Trail junction	10.1 miles, one way.
Avalanche Divide spur trail	11.6 miles, one way.
Schoolroom Glacier	10.8 miles, one way.
Hurricane Pass	11.2 miles, one way.
Sunset Lake (Alaska Basin)	12.4 miles, one way.
Basin Lakes (Alaska Basin)	13.0 miles, one way.

Length from Jenny Lake west shore boat dock to:

Hidden Falls	0.5 miles, one way.
Inspiration Point	1.0 miles, one way.
Cascade Canyon fork	4.6 miles, one way.
Avalanche Divide Trail junction	8.3 miles, one way.
Avalanche Divide spur trail	9.8 miles, one way.
Schoolroom Glacier	9.0 miles, one way.
Hurricane Pass	9.4 miles, one way.
Sunset Lake (Alaska Basin)	10.6 miles, one way.
Basin Lakes (Alaska Basin)	11.2 miles, one way.

Elevation change: Trailhead at 6,785 feet (3,605-foot gain to Hurricane Pass, but a 2,815-foot gain to Basin Lakes).

Trailhead: Located at the southern shore of Jenny Lake at the developed parking area. Or an alternative route from String Lake picnic area.

The Teton Crest Trail is the longest trail along the spine of the Teton Range from Jenny Lake to Teton Pass. It is a long, extended trail of about 31.4 miles and uses a series of other connecting trails featured in this book. The best aspect of this trail is that most of the canyon trails connect to the Teton Crest Trail and any one of them can be joined or left at any time, making numerous route planning possibilities.

PINE MARTEN.

This section of the Teton Crest Trail covers the northern half from Jenny Lake to Alaska Basin. Since this is an extended hike, camping is available in zoned regions in the South Fork Cascade Canyon and in Alaska Basin. This trail section uses the Cascade Canyon, Schoolroom Glacier-South Fork Cascade Canyon and Alaska Basin trails (see respective trails for descriptions).

THE WEST SLOPE OF
THE THREE TETONS.

From Alaska Basin (see Alaska Basin Trail for description) there are several means of departure. One is to hike down and west along Teton Creek into Teton Canyon. This approach exits by vehicle via Driggs, Idaho. Another route heads east to Static Peak and out via Death Canyon (see Death Canyon Trail for description). But the Teton Crest Trail continues south and up to Mount Meek Pass and along the Death Canyon Shelf. For this second section of trail from Alaska Basin to Teton Pass see Teton Crest Trail-South for description.

HANGING CANYON TRAIL
Length from Jenny Lake west shore boat dock to:

Jenny Lake Trail junction	0.15 miles, one way.
Hanging Canyon junction	0.5 miles, one way.
Lake of the Crags	2.4 miles, one way.

Elevation change: Trailhead at 6,785 feet (1,817-foot gain).
Trailhead: Located on the south shore of Jenny Lake at the developed parking area. From this location access is by either foot or boat. Or an alternative foot route from String Lake picnic area.

Hanging Canyon is located in the center of the busiest trail intersection in Grand Teton National Park at Jenny Lake and yet it is relatively unknown and isolated to most hikers. But most mountaineers and climbers are aware of this Shangri-la valley as it accesses a number of classic Teton climbs, including Symmetry Spire and Mount St. John.

This canyon is named for a glacial term which is the result of two glaciers flowing together. The smaller glacier becomes suspended above the main glacier—in this case Cascade Canyon glacier. As they recede a hanging canyon is created. This canyon was left hanging about 1,800 feet above the valley floor. Most hanging canyons as a result have spectacular waterfalls. Hanging Canyon is no exception and has a series of small waterfalls and cascades called Ribbon Falls, originating at Ramshead Lake and Arrowhead Pool.

The start of this trail can be found near the west shore boat dock by locating the Jenny Lake Trail (see Jenny Lake Trail for description). From the four-way junction at Cascade Creek it is about 0.35 miles north on the Jenny Lake Trail, just over a small stream to an unmarked trail heading through thimbleberry, baneberry, monkshood and coniferous trees up slope, away from the lake.

After entering the trees a distinct trail heads toward the main slope into the canyon. It is a steep hike, primarily straight up, with few switchbacks. The views along the way are spectacular of Jenny Lake and the Gros Ventre mountains to the distance. The upper portion of the trail is badly eroded. Be careful not to cause further erosion.

Along the way the trail parallels Ribbon Cascade, a series of small falls and cascades tumbling downward from several higher lakes toward Jenny Lake. The first small lake in the canyon is Arrowhead Pool, followed by Ramshead Lake and at the head of the cirque is the largest of the lakes, Lake of the Crags.

YELLOW BELL.

GLACIER LILY OR
DOGTOOTH VIOLET

AMPHITHEATER-SURPRISE LAKES TRAIL

Length from Lupine Meadows parking area to:

Valley Trail junction	1.4 miles, one way.
Garnet Trail junction	2.7 miles, one way.
Surprise Lake	4.3 miles, one way.
Amphitheater Lake	4.5 miles, one way.
Teton Glacier overlook	4.6 miles, one way.

Elevation change: Trailhead at 6,732 feet (2,966-foot gain).

Trailhead: Located at Lupine Meadows parking area. This gravel road is located just south of Jenny Lake junction and heads across Cottonwood Creek via a wooden bridge to the base of Teewinot Mountain.

This trail is an excellent opportunity to quickly gain elevation and reach treeline in a relatively short hike. It is strenuous, however, with an elevation gain of nearly 3,000 feet in about 4 miles. Along the way the views of the valley and changes in habitat and vegetation provide pauses during the trudge up.

The trail begins from Lupine Meadows parking area, just south of Jenny Lake. During most of the summer wildflowers can be found blooming on the slopes along the trail. In June, beginning on the lower slopes, are arrowleaf balsamroot and spring beauty. As summer progresses these flowers can be found moving up the slope and by late July spring beauties can be found blooming around the lakes.

It is the same with the snowline, moving up slope and by late July most of the snow has freed the lakes of their icy grip.

From Lupine Meadows the trail begins its climb up Avalanche Canyon. At first it follows a lateral moraine to the junction with Valley Trail, then begins a series of switchbacks all the way to the lakes. At Surprise Lake, the first of the two lakes,

the trail begins to somewhat level off. Amphitheater Lake lies just beyond Surprise. The lakes are ringed with limber pine and rocky, gneiss outcroppings.

The best aspect of this hike is actually not the lakes, but the view just above and beyond the lakes. On the edge of a precipitous cliff are

DELTA LAKE FROM AMPHITHEATER OVERLOOK.

incredible views of Delta Lake, below, and Teton Glacier to the northwest. Beyond the glacier is the Grand Teton (13,770 feet) and the peak directly to the west, shadowing the lakes, is Disappointment Peak (11,618 feet).

GARNET CANYON TRAIL

Length from Lupine Meadows parking area to:

Valley Trail junction	1.4 miles, one way.
Garnet Trail junction	2.7 miles, one way.
Meadows	3.7 miles, one way.
Lower Saddle	5.4 miles, one way.

Elevation change: Trailhead at 6,732 feet (4,898-foot gain).

Trailhead: Located at Lupine Meadows parking area. This dirt road is located just south of Jenny Lake and heads across Cottonwood Creek via a wooden bridge to the base of Teewinot Mountain.

AMPHITHEATER LAKE.

Of all the climbers access trails—including Hanging and Avalanche canyons—this is the classic trail. It is primarily a climbers approach to the Lower Saddle from which routes to the Grand, Middle Teton and Teepe Pillar are launched.

The trail uses a portion of the Amphitheater Lake Trail (see Amphitheater-Surprise Lakes Trail for description), originating from Lupine Meadows. This is a well-used, and overused trail during the dry summer months, and if possible should be avoided then.

After a series of Amphitheater-Surprise switchbacks the Garnet Canyon Trail junctions at one of the southern loops. From there it traverses into the canyon past Cleft Falls to a group of large boulders at the Upper Meadows. The trail then begins a series of tight switchbacks to the top of Spalding Falls and a headwall. At this point and beyond requires scrambling and moderate climbing ability, including exposure along the headwall containing Spalding Falls and the crossing of an exposed snowfield. To even reach the Lower Saddle a fixed rope provides assistance to climb up one of the last headwalls.

VALLEY TRAIL-NORTH

Length from Lupine Meadows parking area to:

Amphitheater Trail junction	1.4 miles, one way.
Bradley Lake	2.6 miles, one way.
Taggart Lake	3.4 miles, one way.
Beaver Creek Trail junction	4.5 miles, one way.
Whitegrass trailhead	7.7 miles, one way.

Elevation change: Trailhead at 6,732 feet (48-foot gain, but numerous minor ups and downs).

Trailhead: Located at Lupine Meadows parking area. This gravel road is located just south of Jenny Lake junction and heads across Cottonwood Creek via a wooden bridge to the base of Teewinot Mountain.

The Valley Trail, like the Teton Crest Trail, follows the Teton Range. But the Valley Trail follows along the base of the mountains from Jenny Lake to Teton Village. This description

of the northern section of the Valley Trail begins at Lupine Meadows and ends at Whitegrass Ranger Station. The Valley Trail-South (see Valley Trail-South for description) covers the remaining second half from Whitegrass to Teton Village.

This fascinating 15.1 mile trail covers some unusual terrain and

ON THE TRAIL TO
GARNET CANYON
AMPHITHEATER &
SURPRISE LAKES.

wanders by or through some of the most spectacular lakes and features in Jackson Hole. The trail originated at the turn-of-the-nineteenth-century as a horse trail that lead along the base of the mountains and linked lakes, canyons and dude ranches together. During the 1920s to 1960s there were a number of dude ranches including Lupine Meadows, Danny Ranch, X Quarter Circle X, Highlands, Double Diamond, Half Moon, Trail Ranch, Moose Bell, Whitegrass Ranch, JY Ranch, and Bear Paw. All are defunct now as dude ranches, except for JY Ranch which is a private ranch owned by the Rockefeller family. Most of the ranch buildings, except Lupine Meadows and Highlands which became Park Service housing, were burned for fire exercise by the National Park Service. Along the Valley Trail are the sites of these all-but-forgotten memories of the golden age of dude ranching.

From Lupine Meadows the trail uses the Amphitheater-Surprise Lakes Trail (see Amphitheater-Surprise Lake Trail for description) and junctions just before the main trail begins to switchback. The Valley Trail heads south past Bradley and Taggart lakes before skirting the base of the mountain again for the remaining trail to Whitegrass Ranch and ranger station. It becomes apparent in several locations that shortcuts are possible. If a shortcut is used, keep a sense of direction and know the locations of streams and creeks for possible fordings.

This stretch of trail is relatively easy going, except for the Burned Wagon Gulch section before Bradley Lake. This spot can be detoured by heading south of Lupine Meadows and following the west bank of Cottonwood Creek via the Fabian cabins. This route bypasses Bradley and Taggart lakes, but joins the trail again at the trailhead for the two lakes.

Because most of the trail is directly at the base of the mountains many spots will be marshy and wet from springs. Most of the time the trail circumvents these, but occasionally they cannot be avoided. So, at times expect wet feet. Another hazard is that this trail was developed by horse traffic and as a result in some areas numerous horse trails crisscross, making it complicated to select the best or driest route.

TIMBERED ISLAND HIKE

Length: 2.6 miles, one way.
Elevation change: Trailhead at 6,700 feet (135-foot gain).
Trailhead: Located at the southern end of Timbered Island, 0.8 miles north of the Cottonwood Creek bridge. At the turnoff to the Climber's Ranch and Highlands Park Service housing.

Timbered Island is perhaps the most unusual hike in Grand Teton. It is actually not a trail at all, but a bushwhack through a timbered geologic anomaly.

SULFUR-FLOWERED
BUCKWHEAT.

The start of the hike begins at the turnoff to the Climber's Ranch and Highlands Park Service housing, just south of Jenny Lake. Across the road is the southern tip of Timbered Island. An old road lead around the tip to the back side of the butte where a Park Service dump was located until the early 1990s. The site was primarily used for dumping toxic wastes and the disposal of dead animals, including numerous bears killed intentionally or unintentionally over the years.

Between the Inner Park Road and the butte is an open sagebrush flat, and in this area near the butte is a small marked grave of Alfred G. Sensenbach (1896-1918). He was a World War I ace pilot. He flew biplanes during the war with his close friend Irving Corse, the foreman of the nearby Bar BC Ranch. Sensenbch died tragically shortly after the war and corse arranged to have him buried on the ranch.

By heading north into the trees the central crest can be followed. Numerous game trails crisscross the island. In early summer and late fall this island is a sanctuary for elk. During the day they seek shelter to rest and avoid biting insects and by night they venture out into the sagebrush grassland to forage.

Timbered Island (6,835 feet) was believed to be a glacial esker. Meaning that it was formed under glacial ice by a hole in the glacier where a river or stream running over the ice deposited rock, sand and other debris in the hole. After the glacier melted, a pile was left. Instead this hillock is probably a fractured piece of Teton Fault which became buried, but stuck out of the surrounding plain. Glaciers overrode this projection, carving it down and depositing glacial till around it.

The island is an interesting feature to explore. There are abandoned vehicles, sawmill operations and even bright yellow jerry cans found along the hillock. It is an easy hike and the only difficulty is occasional areas of thick downfall.

LODGEPOLE PINE.

At the north end after leaving the lodgepole trees it is possible to connect with an old road that leads to Jenny Lake. The road has been reclaimed, but a faint outline is visible and a three-quarter mile hike ends at the Jenny Lake road turnoff.

BRADLEY-TAGGART LAKES TRAIL

Length from Bradley-Taggart parking area to:

Bradley-Taggart Lake trail junction	0.3 miles, one way.
North Trail:	
Figure-eight cutoff trail	1.2 miles, one way.
Avalanche Trail junction	2.4 miles, one way.
Bradley Lake	1.6 miles, one way.
Bradley-Taggart Lakes loop	4.8 miles, loop.
South Trail:	
Valley Trail junction	1.3 miles, one way.
Taggart Lake	2.2 miles, one way.

Elevation change: Trailhead at 6,631 feet (391-foot gain to Bradley Lake and a 271-foot gain to Taggart Lake).

Trailhead: Begins at the Bradley and Taggart lakes parking area located 3.8 miles south of Jenny Lake junction or 2.9 miles northwest of Moose on the Inner Park Road.

Outside of the Jenny Lake area Bradley-Taggart Lakes Trail is probably the second most popular hike in Grand Teton National Park, and on summer days the parking area can be packed with vehicles and hikers gearing up for an excursion to the two small lakes at the base of the Teton Range.

The trail system among these two lakes may seem complicated, but it is essentially a figure-eight. The lower loop is a large O with a smaller northern loop connecting to Bradley Lake. For this reason a number of routes and hiking opportunities become available.

The first stretch of the trail wanders through a sagebrush meadow into aspen and lodgepole stands. At the first junction the north trail leads to Bradley lake via the eastern side of the figure-eight. Thus the south trail leads to Taggart then Bradley lakes via the lower and western portion of the figure-eight. Either

RARE SKATING ON
BRADLEY LAKE.

direction, clockwise or counterclockwise, provides great views and an excellent route.

For hikers accessing Avalanche Canyon, however, the northern route to the cutoff portion of the figure-eight is a shortcut to Taggart and is the quickest route to Avalanche Canyon Trail junction (see Avalanche Canyon Trail for description).

TAGGART LAKE.

Most of the Bradley-Taggart trail wanders over the hummocky topography of glacial moraines, and glacial erratics are found strewn throughout the area. Both lakes are the result of glaciers. Bradley was formed by a glacier spilling from Garnet Canyon. While Taggart Lake is the result of a glacier from Avalanche Canyon.

The rolling, hummocky terrain was covered in a dense lodgepole pine and subalpine fir forest prior to a forest fire in the mid 1980s. Since then the moraines were exposed, except for burned skeleton tree trunks. New vegetation has slowly reestablished. First with alders, Ceanothus and buffaloberry, then young sapling lodgepoles. The skeleton trees may last nearly a century as the new forest slowly matures over the same time.

The lakes were named by the 1872 Hayden Survey. James Stevenson, commanding the southern portion of the Yellowstone expedition was the first official explorer to enter Jackson's Hole—as it was known then. Photographer William H. Jackson accompanied the group and made the first photographs. They named the lakes in honor of their chief geologist, Frank Howe Bradley, and assistant geologist, William Rush Taggart.

Winter brings another aspect to this trail. The road is usually plowed up to this parking area and from there it is possible to ski the entire trail loop. Both lakes are frozen over and a layer of snow gives them the appearance of snowy fields. Chickadees are a common winter inhabitant and they can be distinguished by their chick-a-dee-dee song. Gray jays and their look alike cousins, the Clark's nutcracker, also are common.

AVALANCHE CANYON TRAIL

Length from Bradley-Taggart parking area to:

Taggart Lake	1.6 miles, one way.
Avalanche Trail junction	2.4 miles, one way.
Fork of Taggart Creek	4.2 miles, one way.
Shoshoko Falls	4.9 miles, one way.
Lake Taminah	5.1 miles, one way.

Elevation change: Trailhead at 6,631 feet (2,424-foot gain).
Trailhead: Begins at the Bradley and Taggart lakes parking area located 3.8 miles south of Jenny Lake junction of 2.9 miles northwest of Moose on the Inner Park Road.

This mountaineering trail is not official, but it is a highly used climbers trail reaching into the east front of the Teton Range to a double waterfall and a small subalpine lake.

This trail begins by using the Bradley-Taggart Lakes Trail (see Bradley-Taggart Lakes Trail for description). The trail to Taggart must first be taken, and on the moraine separating the two lakes the trail junctions with the Avalanche Canyon Trail. It is an unmarked trail but it heads west along the southern slope of the moraine into and up the canyon.

The trail stays to the north of the creek and at the fork of Taggart Creek begins to cross several talus slopes. Shoshoko Falls becomes visible by then. It is a double waterfall a little over a hundred feet high. The stream originates from Lake Taminah. It is possible to scramble up to the lake along a talus slope on the northside of the canyon. But the approach is somewhat treacherous.

Most of the water feeding Lake Taminah and Taggart Lake is derived from snowmelt. The waterfall roars in the spring with snowmelt and diminishes later in the summer.

TAGGART CREEK.

Hiking Moose-Teton Village

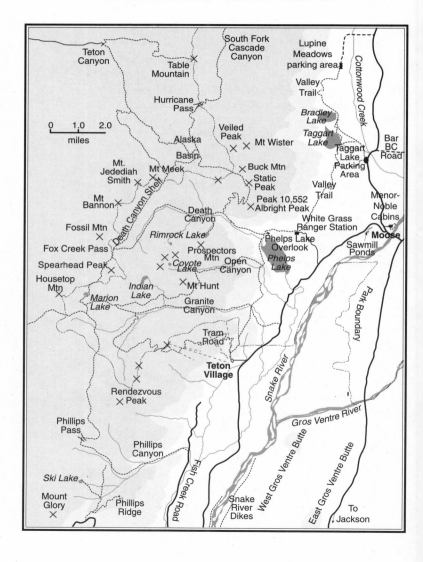

MOOSE-TETON VILLAGE

Moose and Teton Village lie in the heart of Jackson Hole. It is a region which encompasses the center of this broad valley with the Snake River flowing through it. On its western edge the Teton Range rises abruptly and dominantly, overshadowing the valley.

Within this region of extremes is a diversity of hiking terrain. This area possesses sheer mountain cliffs, deep glacial etched canyons, backcountry lakes, ancient outwash plains and braided river beds.

WINTER IN THE TETONS.

The lower elevations along the Snake River provide hikers with early and late season hiking, but mountain canyons and passes remain snow-covered until mid to lake July and again by early to late October winter snows creep back.

There is history here, too. From early pioneers who established the first ferry across the Snake River to the first dude ranch in the valley. And the monumental cabin where citizens decided to take a stance and preserve it all. These places are all available for the hiker to explorer.

Another area of exploration is Teton Village and Rendezvous Peak. Beyond winter skiing the mountain opens up a region of hikes and immediate access to subalpine terrain, including wildflower meadows, cirque lakes and windswept summits. While on the opposite scale the Snake River provides easygoing walk-the-dog type hikes along the dikes of the river. While other river trails provide access to fishing holes or wildlife ponds.

BAR BC RANCH TRAIL 🚲

Length from ranch gate to:

dining hall	0.2 miles, one way.
beaver ponds	0.7 miles, one way.
swimming hole	1.2 miles, one way.

Elevation change: Trailhead at 6,568 feet (70-foot loss).

Trailhead: The turn off for the ranch is located on the Inner Park Road, just north of the Cottonwood Creek bridge. The gravel road is the southern portion of the RKO Road, and it is 1.8 miles to the trailhead and parking area at the ranch gate.

The Bar BC Ranch has been a well kept secret in the heart of Jackson Hole and is one of the few remaining remnants of

early history and dude ranching in the valley. The ranch was homesteaded about 1911, by Philadelphians Struthers Burt and Dr. Horace Carncross, giving the ranch its moniker—BC. Burt, a bestselling author, had been a partner in the JY Ranch, the first dude ranch, and had fallen in love with the val-

BAR BC RANCH.

ley. He enticed a new partner, a prominent psychiatrist, to homestead and develop the dude ranch. With their connections to the wealthy and social elite of Philadelphia and

Princeton they encouraged them to visit Jackson Hole for the summers.

During the Bar BC's heyday of the 1920s and 30s it boasted a swimming pond—complete with diving board, a recreation center, two dining halls, a trap shoot, a large and impressive library, horse corrals, airstrip with airplane hangar, its own water powered electric generating system, fish hatchery, rodeo grounds and fleet of touring cars. Music, costume balls, plays and dancing went on throughout the nights.

Even Struthers Burt's wife, Katherine, attracted her Hollywood friends of the silent film era, including Tom Mix, and John Wayne's first film was shot here. Over the years, others have been attracted here too. Walt Disney spent part of the summer filming otters along the Snake River. Sally Carrighar wrote her book, *A Day at Teton Marsh*, just south of the ranch. Members of the Rockefeller family spent summers fishing and horseback riding. And even President Jimmy Carter spent a day fishing along the bank of the river, sending secret servicemen to town for buckets of Kentucky fried chicken.

By about 1930 the Burt's moved to Pacific Creek and the ranch was eventually sold to the National Park Service with the stipulation that his new partner, Irving Corse, and wife could live on the ranch for the remainder of their lives. Irv Corse divorced his first wife and remarried. Margaretta "Maggie" Corse, his second wife spent her summers on the ranch until her death in the late 1980s. Irv Corse committed suicide in the 1950s.

Before Mrs. Corse's death she stated "the Park Service would rather see this place bulldozed, than preserve it." The Park Service did not make any attempts at a crucial time before or after her death to protect or preserve the Bar BC Ranch. It is now in ruins, most of the buildings are either gone or their roofs have collapsed from the weight of heavy snow. But walking through the ranch is to relive its history of past glorious times.

ANTELOPE
BITTERBRUSH.

The hike begins at the parking area next to the gate on a

bench overlooking the ranch. Take notice at the gate, however, that the ranch may or may not be open to the public due to politics of the National Park Service. From the gate the road drops steeply to the river bottom and to the north, hidden among narrowleaf cottonwoods, is the generator building. A diversion ditch from Cottonwood Creek diverted water across the sagebrush flats, skirting the southern tip of Timbered Island. This ditch is still visible by the growth of cottonwood

SNAKE RIVER
OVERLOOK.

trees along the edge. The water entered a pipe near the bench, then dropped steeply to the small hydroelectric generator. Near the generator was a barn that was removed in the early 1990s.

At the base of the hill, to the south is the horse corral and tack room where each dude kept their saddle and horse equipment. Also at the base of the hill, at the edge of the willows, is the site of the main, or foreman's, house. It was the only winterized building on the ranch, but the house burned during a winter fire and the occupants barely escaped with their lives.

The old road heads south through dilapidated cabins to the old dining hall, now recognizable by the exposed fireplace. A wing connected to the dining hall housed an extensive library, including numerous books authored by the Burts. Behind the building is the ruins of the bath house, with remains of its coal-fired boiler. This building also burned down years ago in a fire. The small single or two room cabins scattered around the ranch were guest cabins.

Opposite the road from the dining hall is a large depression, the remains of the swimming pond that was once filled by the spent water from the hydroelectric generator. Between the pond and the river is the deteriorating log recreation hall, where costume balls, all night dances to weddings were held. On the other side of the recreation hall was the trap shoot where fragments of clay pigeons still litter the ground.

The last two large buildings to the south and west was the home of Mrs. Corse and the airplane hangar of her husband's World War I biplane. The road after leaving the ranch buildings continues south through the sagebrush flat, that once served as a landing strip, to a series of beaver ponds along the river. The road ends at what was once an old campground and the remains of the fish hatchery. The foundation of the hatchery manager's residence is still visible as well as some of the concrete fish runs. Just beyond the house foundation to the west is a spring fed pond, a popular swimming hole.

The Bar BC Ranch is an exciting and fascinating area to explore. But it does have its hazards that should not be ignored. Probably the greatest hazard are the numerous Uinta ground squirrel and badger holes that riddle the ground. It is easy to place a foot into one of these and twist or break an ankle. Another hazard to lookout for are the numerous boards that are lying about from the dismantling of some of the buildings. These boards often have rusty nails protruding from them and a nail into a foot is a serious concern for tetanus. The last major hazard to avoid is to not enter the buildings, but it is safe to peer into them. Rotten floor boards and collapsing roofs can go at any moment.

UINTA GROUND
SQUIRREL.

MENOR-NOBLE TRAIL

Length: 1.0 mile loop.
Elevation change: Trailhead at 6,460 feet (no perceptual elevation change).
Trailhead: The parking area is located at the Chapel of the Transfiguration, north of the Moose entrance station. Another approach is by hiking north from the Moose visitor center along the shore of the Snake River.

GOLDEN-MANTLED
GROUND SQUIRREL.

The Menor's Ferry and Maude Noble cabin trail is a short but interesting trail through a piece of Jackson Hole history.

During the summer most of the buildings are open to the public and the ferry is sometimes in operation. In winter the buildings are boarded up, but it is a popular snowshoe hike among the outbuildings.

The trail begins in the parking area of the Chapel of the Transfiguration. The chapel was built in 1925 by local ranchers and dude ranchers for the convenience of a shorter ride for Sunday worship, as opposed to riding to Jackson where the nearest church was located. With donated timber and labor they sited the church with its large picture window over the altar directly at the Grand Teton. The church today is a favorite for weddings, and on a summer Saturday the bell at the entrance arch rings out the ceremonies.

Opposite the parking area from the chapel is the trail to the river and Menor's Ferry. The first cabin on the left is occasionally used for displays, but usually it is vacant. The next building, a whitewashed log cabin, was originally built in 1892 by homesteader William (Bill) Menor. He discovered an enterprise along this section of the river—one of the few locations along the Snake where the river is in one channel instead of numerous braided streams—to establish a ferry for horse riders, walkers and wagons. In one room he also had a general store and sold supplies and staples to his river crossing clients.

The ferry is propelled entirely by the current of the river. By shifting the direction of the pontoons the river current pushes against the side of the pontoons and the ferry moves across the river, aided by the use of pulleys on a fixed cable.

MERGANSER.

The trail continues to a display of early transportation in the valley, including old dude ranch carriages and stage coaches. These items and the preservation of this area was accomplished by the Jackson Hole Preserve, started and funded by the Rockefeller family.

As the trail enters the large black cottonwood and narrowleaf cottonwood stand there is a small, low roofed log cabin known as the Maude Noble cabin. She was an early Jackson Hole character. Maude purchased Menor's Ferry in 1918 and moved her cabin from nearby Cottonwood Creek to this site. She continued to operate the ferry until 1927 when a bridge made it obsolete and she sold to Rockefeller's Snake River Land Company. But before she moved an important meeting was held in her home in 1923. Maude with other influential Jackson Hole residents met with then Yellowstone superintendent, Horace Albright to discuss the possible preservation of Jackson Hole. From that meeting Albright eventually met up with philanthropist John D. Rockefeller, Jr. in 1929 who formed the Snake River Land Company and purchased valley property, including the Noble cabin. After years of government delays Rockefeller eventually donated these holdings in 1943, forming Jackson Hole Monument. By 1950 the monument was incorporated into the present Grand Teton National Park.

From the cabin the trail loops back via a dirt road to the parking area. However, it is possible to return to the visitor center along a path by the Snake River (located behind the cabin) or by walking through Park Service housing to the back entrance of the visitor center.

SCHWABACHER LANDING
Length: 0.6 mile, one way.
Elevation change: Trailhead at 6,554 feet (no perceptual elevation change).
Trailhead: The turnoff is located 3.0 miles north of Moose junction on U.S. Highway 89. A narrow dirt road heads west and down an embankment onto the river flood plain. At the end of the short road is the trailhead.

Schwabacher's Landing is a jewel of a location for early morning or exploratory walks. The land was originally a part of the Schwabacher property, but they sold their ranch to the Rockefeller's Snake River Land Company and the family relocated to Pinedale. The road was then used as a landing and launching site for rafting and boating on the Snake River until recently. In the early years the channel at the trailhead had a

BEAVER.

steady flow, but in subsequent years the channel shifted and the water has become land locked. Given another shift during spring flooding and this channel could become active again.

LEOPARD LILY.

The channel at the trailhead has also been immortalized in cinema. Alan Ladd in the film *Shane* rode across the stream on horseback with young Joey, played by Brandon de Wilde, chasing after him on his way to the final shoot-out with Jack Palance's character, Jack Wilson. At this same location Charleton Heston and Brian Keith had a knockout fight in the film *The Mountain Men*. Walt Disney, too, filmed captive river otters frolicking here in the channel.

From the parking area an unofficial fishermen's trail heads north between the edge of an abandoned river channel and a river bench. The trail then leads to a stand of blue spruce at the edge of a small pond. This pond acts as a reflecting pool against the Teton Range and some of the most prominent photographs of the Tetons have been photographed from this location. For this reason photographers can be found here at sunrise trying to capture the day's first light on the Grand Teton.

From the reflecting pond the trail climbs to the edge of a bench and continues along its edge to the beaver pond. The pond once held a large and thriving community of beavers, but has since silted in. This old pond once had numerous canals branching out into the surrounding forest. The canals were used to search for food. As all of the aspen were cut near the pond, beaver had to search farther and farther away for more sources. The canals provided protection during their forays and also provided a means to transport heavy and otherwise bulky branches cut from fallen trees. The branches were then taken to a deep section of the main pond and secured to the bottom for winter use when the pond's surface froze over, that otherwise limited their foraging ability .

The trail fizzles out at the beaver ponds, but it is possible to explore the area by bushwhacking either down into the river plain or by continuing north through the sagebrush plain.

BLACKTAIL BUTTE

Length: 2.3 miles, one way.
Elevation change: Trailhead at 6,525 feet (1,150-foot gain).
Trailhead: Located 0.9 miles north of the Moose junction on Highway 89/187. A paved spur road leads to a parking area at the base of a limestone cliff.

Blacktail Butte is a geological anomaly in the middle of Jackson Hole. Glaciers, dating 15,000 to 250,000 years ago, filled and flowed down the valley, overriding Blacktail Butte. The flowing ice polished and formed the Madison limestone butte into its present boat-shape form.

The 1872 Hayden Survey party named the butte for the blacktail (mule) deer that were plentiful there. Survey geologist Frank Bradley reported: "Near the butte, large areas of sage had been burned off, and the grasses had grown up densely, forming fine pasturage; and on these, we again encountered antelope."

Historically fires swept across the butte and kept it relatively barren. That was how the Hayden party discovered the butte. But today, because of fire suppression, the butte is forested. As a result, wildlife use has changed from mule deer and antelope to elk and moose. In early spring or late fall, they or their signs often can be spotted in the ravines.

Access to the butte is on the northwest corner, 0.9 miles north of Moose Junction and just off the highway. A parking area is provided at the base of the vertical limestone wall. This wall is a popular practice rock for climbing. Twenty or more difficult routes test top-roped climbers on the 5.9 to 5.12c classed climbs.

WINTER IN MOOSE.

Just south of the wall is a trail and staircase that provide top roping access for climbs. This trail also leads to the top of

Blacktail Butte (7,688 feet), after a strenuous 1,150-foot gain. From the top is an excellent view of the Teton Range and the surrounding Jackson Hole.

Another hike from the parking area skirts the western base of the butte. This trail leads directly south from the parking area and follows an old road, irrigation ditch and several isolated ravines. Some have springs, and the ravines are surprisingly cool and moist with lush vegetation and the perfect hideaway on a hot summer day. The trail continues to the southern end of the butte, still skirting its edge, and eventually joins the Gros Ventre-Kelly road near the campground.

WINTER ALONG THE
SNAKE RIVER.

Trails to the summit of the butte also are accessible from the southern end. The southern portion of what was Mormon Row road, across from the Gros Ventre campground, is the trailhead for the southern routes up the butte. This access is longer, but the gradient is not as steep.

SAWMILL PONDS TRAIL
Length: 0.7 miles, one way.
Elevation change: Trailhead at 6,480 feet (no perceptual elevation change).
Trailhead: Located 1.2 miles south of Moose on the Moose-Wilson road. A large turnout and parking space is available on the bench overlooking the wildlife ponds.

For viewing wildlife and a great morning or evening stroll, this is the trail. It is easily accessible for all age levels and is a rewarding walk along a series of wildlife ponds.

The trailhead is located south of Moose on the Moose-Wilson road. The parking area is perched on a bench overlooking Sawmill Ponds. From this first location it is possible to immediately discover if there is wildlife activity.

Sawmill Ponds were originally called Huckleberry Springs, and it is the source of Reserve Creek which flows along the bench and parallels the Moose-Wilson road. Beaver have formed dams along the creek, creating ponds and habitat for a variety of wildlife, including moose, otter, mink, muskrat, cranes and nesting waterfowl.

Sawmill Pond is in reference to Al Young's sawmill which he operated here between 1920 and 1929.

The trail from Sawmill Ponds overlook heads south following an old road and an old river bench. This old road lead to the Moose Bell Ranch, an early dude ranch with its own airplane landing strip out on the flat sagebrush plain. The dude ranch was purchased by the National Park Service and the buildings were moved in the early 1980s. Those buildings now make up the core of the C-V school, farther south on the Moose-Wilson road.

Just south of the landing strip was the home of Malcom Forbs, millionaire, entrepreneur and publisher of *Forbs* magazine. This home, too, was purchased by the National Park Service and moved in the mid 1980s.

VALLEY TRAIL-SOUTH

Length from Teton Village to:

Granite Canyon Trail junction	2.4 miles, one way.
Open Canyon Trail junction	4.6 miles, one way.
Death Canyon Trail junction	5.8 miles, one way.
Phelps Lake Overlook	6.5 miles, one way.
Whitegrass trailhead	7.4 miles, one way.

Elevation change: Trailhead at 6,311 feet (469-foot gain).
Trailhead: The trailhead begins at the Teton Village clock tower and heads north past the east side of the Best Western Hotel.

This section of the Valley Trail is the southern continuation of its northern counterpart, which begins at Lupine Meadows and meets this section at Whitegrass trailhead and ranger station (see Valley Trail-North for description).

The entire Valley Trail follows the base of the Teton Range for its 15.1 mile length. But this section incorporates more up and down as the trail moves in and out of canyon entrances.

The trail leaves Teton Village and heads north through aspen and lodgepoles. This initial stretch is heavily used by horse riders from the village. But by Granite Canyon the trail thins out and is not as heavily used.

From Granite Canyon the trail circumvents the base of the mountain to Phelps Lake. A problem along the way are occasional wet springs or seeps at the mouths of Open and Death canyons. The trail then climbs over Phelps Lake moraine, through Douglas firs and the Phelps Lake Overlook to Whitegrass trailhead.

LARKSPUR.

PHELPS LAKE TRAIL

Length from Whitegrass ranger station to:

Phelps Lake Overlook	0.9 miles, one way.
Phelps Lake Trail junction	1.8 miles, one way.
Death Canyon patrol cabin	3.7 miles, one way.

Elevation change: Trailhead at 6,780 feet (422-foot gain to the overlook).

Trailhead: Starts at the Whitegrass ranger station parking area, just off the Moose-Wilson Road. The turnoff to Whitegrass is 3.1 miles south of Moose and another 1.5 miles to the end of the road at the parking area and trailhead.

Phelps Lake overlook is an interesting hike anytime during the summer or fall and a moderate ski tour during winter.

From the trailhead the trail gradually ascends through a lodgepole and subalpine forest. After a short distance from the parking area the trail junctions with the Valley Trail (see Valley Trail-North or Valley Trail-South for descriptions).

The Valley Trail in this area was heavily used by hikers and horse riders staying at the Whitegrass Ranch, located about a mile northeast. The dude ranch during its heyday was operated by Frank Galey, a heavy gin drinker who conducted cocktail "hour", which began in the afternoon and lasted into the early morning hours. During that time high stake card games, including poker and bridge also were played. His independent manner irked the Park Service, who promptly burned and bull-dozed the dude ranch after his death in the mid 1980s.

The Valley Trail junction has since received less traffic and some of the confusing horse trails have disappeared. Parts of the trail to the overlook are lined by small streams and seeps which support lush growth of thimbleberries, mountain alder and false hellebore. Just before the overlook the site suddenly becomes drier, supporting aspen and Douglas fir.

The overlook, an overgrown glacial lateral moraine, pro-vides a spectacular view of Phelps Lake and southeast out across the valley to the Gros Ventre buttes. The lake was named by members of the 1872 Hayden Survey in honor of a trapper who trapped and hunted in this area for years. Although not much more is known about him. Along the eastern shore of Phelps Lake is a small set of cabins. This is the old JY Ranch first home-steaded in 1908 as the first dude ranch in Jackson Hole. Owen Wister, author of *The Virginian*, was one of its more famous guests. It was later purchased in 1927 by John D. Rockefeller, Jr. and has been held by the family ever since. However, 1221 acres surrounding the ranch were donated by the Rockefellers to medical research in 1983. In a com-plicated land swap the property was eventually sold to the Park Service. Only the cabins and a few acres around them now remain in the Rockefeller family holdings.

PHELPS LAKE
OVERLOOK.

The trail continues down the steep face of the moraine via switchbacks to Phelps Lake and the continuing trail to Death Canyon. Just beyond the base of the moraine is a junction. This trail leads to the lake and the inlet for fishing access.

The trail into Death Canyon (see Death Canyon Trail for

description) or Open Canyon (see Open Canyon Trail for description) are rewarding trail hikes, and they are just as interesting geologically as Cascade Canyon. During early July this is perhaps one of the best canyons for wildflowers, and it also is noted for its abundant wildlife.

DEATH CANYON TRAIL

Length from Whitegrass ranger station to:

Phelps Lake Overlook	0.9 miles, one way.
Phelps Lake Trail junction	1.8 miles, one way.
Death Canyon patrol cabin	3.7 miles, one way.
Peak 10,552 trail junction	3.7 miles, one way.
Fox Creek Pass	8.6 miles, one way.

Elevation change: Trailhead at 6,780 feet (2,280-foot gain).
Trailhead: Starts at the Whitegrass ranger station parking area, just off the Moose-Wilson Road. The turnoff to Whitegrass is 3.1 miles south of Moose and it is another 1.5 miles from the junction to the end of the road where the parking and trailhead are located.

The best aspect of a hike up Death Canyon is the discovery of an interesting formation at the head of the canyon. The

MULE DEER.

Death Canyon Shelf runs over 2.5 miles long and appears as a man-made terraced wall from which water streams down.

This trail begins at Whitegrass ranger station and utilizes the Phelps Lake Trail (see Phelps Lake Trail for description) to the mouth of Death Canyon. At this point another trail junctions here. The Open Canyon Trail and Valley Trail (see either for description) head south along the base of the Teton Range.

From the meadow at the canyon's mouth the trail begins its steady ascent up the canyon. At the switchbacks are great views of Phelps Lake and the valley beyond. But above the switchbacks the canyon becomes constricted, cutting off most views down the valley.

At the Death Canyon patrol cabin is a resting area and a trail junction to Peak 10,552 (see Peak 10,552 for description), Static Peak, Buck Mountain, and beyond to Alaska Basin.

Continuing from the patrol cabin the Death Canyon Trail proceeds upstream and makes a couple of stream crossings via bridges. At the base of Death Canyon Shelf the trail curves south and follows along its base to the head of the drainage at Fox Creek Pass.

From the shelf numerous springs weep from the sedimentary rock wall and run down into the creek. Along the top of the shelf is the Teton Crest Trail (see Teton Crest Trail for description) which parallels Death Canyon Trail below.

At Fox Creek Pass is a four-way trail junction. The Teton Crest Trail runs north-south. The trail heading west (its junction, however, is on the south side of the pass) enters Fox Creek drainage and emerges into the Idaho side of the Teton Range.

LONG-LEAVED
PHLOX.

RIMROCK LAKE

Length from Whitegrass ranger station to:

Phelps Lake Overlook	0.9 miles, one way.
Phelps Lake Trail junction	1.8 miles, one way.
Death Canyon patrol cabin	3.7 miles, one way.
Death Canyon bridge	4.3 miles, one way.
Rimrock Lake	5.2 miles, one way.

Elevation change: Trailhead at 6,780 feet (3,136-foot gain).
Trailhead: Starts at the Whitegrass ranger station parking area, just off the Moose-Wilson Road. The turnoff to Whitegrass is 3.1 miles south of Moose and it is another 1.5 miles from the junction to the end of the road where the parking and trailhead are located.

Rimrock Lake is truly a magical lake in a magical location with its head among the clouds. This trip is not an ordinary hike, but requires an amount of mountaineering skill to maneuver through and over cliff exposure and snowfields.

The approach to Rimrock Lake utilizes the Phelps Lake and Death Canyon trails (see each for descriptions). About 0.6 miles up the canyon from the patrol cabin is a bridge that provides a crossing to the south bank of the stream. From the bridge to the lake it is a 1,900-foot climb and a path may not always be discernible. Often a trail is obliterated by moving talus or by winter snow. Immediately visible from the bridge to the south is the drainage from Rimrock Lake. To the east of the drainage is a possible scramble, but it does require roped protection on the exposed cliffs near the top.

Another route immediately off the bridge and on the west side of the drainage wanders through coniferous trees up a talus gully that parallels the lakes drainage. Rock scrambling is required at the top of the gully when following the eastward trending ridge to the lake. This route is made extremely difficult with late season snow and ice in the gully. Since this is a north facing slope there may be remnants into August.

MUSK THISTLE.

The lake is a small cirque and fed by snowfields from the headwall. The area is extremely fragile since the subalpine plants and wildflowers growing around it only have a short, limited season to grow, bloom and reproduce. Take extra care not to disturb this fragile site.

PEAK 10,552 TRAIL
(renamed Albright Peak)
Length from Whitegrass ranger station to:

Phelps Lake Overlook	0.9 miles, one way.
Phelps Lake Trail junction	1.8 miles, one way.
Death Canyon patrol cabin	3.7 miles, one way.
Peak 10,552	6.4 miles, one way.
Static Peak	7.4 miles, one way.

Elevation change: Trailhead at 6,780 feet (3,772-foot gain).
Trailhead: Starts at the Whitegrass ranger station parking area, just off the Moose-Wilson Road. The turnoff to Whitegrass is

3.1 miles south of Moose and it is another 1.5 miles from the junction to the end of the road where the parking and trailhead are located.

Peak 10,552 (pronounced ten-five-fifty-two) has been a well-know peak and one of the easiest peaks in the range to conquer. Its name is reflective of its height—elevation 10,552 feet. Its name, however, was changed to Albright Peak in the early 1990s by the National Park Service to honor one of their own—Horace Albright, the first park service superintendent of Yellowstone National Park.

To arrive at this spur trail of the Death Canyon Trail portions of the Phelps Lake and Death Canyon trails are used (see each for description). At Death Canyon patrol cabin the trail junctions. The trail heading north begins the arduous 2,600-foot climb up to the peak. The entire climb is on the western, or backside, of Peak 10,552 and offers no spectacular views other than of Prospectors Mountain (11,241 feet) to the south of the canyon.

Near the top of the switchbacks is a false summit or point. This overlooks the canyon and provides the first views of the valley, but is not the actual summit itself. Continue on and the trail contours along the pyramidal summit of 10,552. From the main trail there are several game-like trails which scramble and make their way to the top.

From the summit are incredible views of Jackson Hole. In the foreground is the steep, but rounded east slope of Peak 10,552. At its base is Phelps Lake and the horseshoe-shaped moraine.

The trail continues from Peak 10,552 northward to Static Peak (11,303 feet), which also is an easy scramble to the summit. The next peak is Buck Mountain (11,938 feet). Buck Mountain is a more difficult peak to climb, and is considered a mountaineering peak. Many hikers have underestimated this moun-

DEATH CANYON
FROM PEAK 10,552.

tain and lost their lives on it due to exposure or from fatal falls.

Past the west slope of Buck the trail crosses out of Grand Teton National park and enters Targhee National Forest into Alaska Basin and junctions with the Teton Crest Trail (see Teton Crest Trail for description).

STATIC PEAK TRAIL

Length from Whitegrass ranger station to:

Phelps Lake Overlook	0.9 miles, one way.
Phelps Lake Trail junction	1.8 miles, one way.
Death Canyon patrol cabin	3.7 miles, one way.
Peak 10,552	6.4 miles, one way.
Static Peak	7.4 miles, one way.

Elevation change: Trailhead at 6,780 feet (4,523-foot gain).

Trailhead: Starts at the Whitegrass ranger station parking area, just off the Moose-Wilson Road. The turnoff to Whitegrass is 3.1 miles south of Moose and it is another 1.5 miles from the junction to the end of the road where the parking and trailhead are located.

Static Peak (11,303 feet), like its neighbor Peak 10,552, is easily accessible by foot even though it is a strenuous hike.

This peak is accessed by the same trail to Peak 10,552 (see Peak 10,552 Trail for description). It begins at Whitegrass ranger station, past Phelps Lake, up Death Canyon to the patrol cabin and junction, then a series of switchbacks up the backside of Peak 10,552.

After the summit of Peak 10,552 the trail continues north. Again an official trail does not lead to the summit, but a number of game-like trails make their way to the top. The views, of course, are stupendous of the valley and of Buck Mountain (11,938 feet), clearly visibly to the north.

OPEN CANYON TRAIL

Length from Whitegrass ranger station to:

Phelps Lake Overlook	0.9 miles, one way.

Phelps Lake Trail junction	1.8 miles, one way.
Open Canyon trail junction	2.4 miles, one way.
Mount Hunt Divide	6.8 miles, one way.
Granite Canyon trail junction	10.2 miles, one way.

Elevation change: Trailhead at 6,780 feet (2,960-foot gain to Mount Hunt Divide, but a 1,550-foot gain to Granite Canyon). Trailhead: Starts at the Whitegrass ranger station, just off the Moose-Wilson Road. The turnoff to Whitegrass is 3.1 miles south of Moose and another 1.5 miles from the junction to the end of the road where the parking and trailhead are located.

PORCUPINE.

Of all the major Teton front range canyons, Open Canyon is one of the toughest, steepest and less traveled. It is primarily a mountaineers trail accessing climbs in the Mount Hunt region.

The first two mile stretch of trail utilizes the Phelps Lake Trail (see Phelps Lake Trail for description) to the mouth of Death Canyon (see Death Canyon Trail for description). At the trail junction Open Canyon heads due south over a bridge and along Phelps Lake to another junction at the mouth of Open Canyon. This area is crisscrossed with horse trails from the JY Ranch, and trail finding can be confusing. Keep a bearing in mind when choosing a trail.

From Phelps Lake the trail begins a steady climb up Open Canyon via numerous switchbacks to Mount Hunt Divide. Mount Hunt (10,783 feet) is to the west and views of Granite Canyon are to the south of Rendezvous.

It is all down hill into Granite Canyon from Mount Hunt Divide, but the descent is to the west, to the upper regions of Granite. The trail merges with the Granite Canyon Trail (see Granite Canyon Trail for description) between Marion Lake and the upper Granite Canyon patrol cabin. From the junction it is possible to continue up the canyon to join the Teton Crest Trail at Marion Lake, or it is possible to connect with the Rendezvous Mountain Trail (see Rendezvous Mountain Trail for description) while heading out along the Granite Canyon Trail.

GRANITE CANYON TRAIL 🔺 ⛷

Length from Granite Canyon Trailhead to:

Valley Trail junction	1.5 miles, one way.
Mouth of Granite Canyon	1.7 miles, one way.
Granite Canyon patrol cabin	6.0 miles, one way.
Rendezvous Mountain Trail junction	6.0 miles, one way.
Open Canyon Trail junction	6.8 miles, one way.
Teton Crest Trail junction	8.0 miles, one way.
Marion Lake	8.7 miles, one way.

Elevation change: Trailhead at 6,370 feet. (2,860-foot gain to Marion Lake).

Trailhead: Located at the Granite Canyon parking area, 2.0 miles north of the Teton Village junction on the Moose-Wilson Road, shortly after the pavement ends. Or it is possible to drive 6.0 miles south of Moose on the same road to the trailhead.

FAIRY SLIPPER.

Granite Canyon can be called an all-purpose trail. It provides access to wildflower meadows, a subalpine lake, climbing points, mountain summits, and an aerial tram. This trail is, perhaps, best known as the exit for the aerial tram and Rendezvous Mountain Trail.

LOWER GRANITE CREEK CABIN BEFORE ITS COLLAPSE.

The trail begins in a sagebrush and aspen meadow at the foot of the canyon. During June this stretch of trail is lined with wildflowers, including arrowleaf balsamroot, woodland stars, larkspur, phlox and fairy slipper orchids.

As the trail approaches the canyon it enters the lodgepole forest and junctions, at first with horse trails leading to Teton Village, then with the Valley Trail (see Valley Trail for description). The Valley Trail is more commonly used as a return route to Teton Village for hikes down from the tram.

From the junction the trail crosses Granite Creek via a couple of bridges. The Valley Trail (see Valley Trail-South for description) does continue north to Phelps Lake. The trail north, however, is crisscrossed with horse trails leading to and from the JY Ranch. Watch for the main trail and keep a sense of direction if this trail is selected.

Just past the bridges the trail junctions to Granite Canyon and follows the creek upstream. At the mouth of the canyon, south of the trail between two channels of Granite Creek and somewhat hidden, is the lower patrol cabin. It was a hub of activity for years. The historical cabin was abandoned for unknown reasons by the Park Service in the mid 1980s and heavy snowfall in 1996 collapsed the structure.

Granite Canyon is very steep sloped and in several locations avalanche paths are obvious. And in other locations rock fall and talus slopes mark the valley floor. These are indicators of more recent events. Glaciers, ending 9,000 to 12,000 years ago originally carved the canyon, but Granite Creek has etched the canyon further.

MARION LAKE.

The first major landmark up the canyon is the upper patrol cabin. This cabin is used primarily during the summer by the trail crew. Three creeks and drainages—the North, Middle, and South forks of Granite Creek—merge in this vicinity. The Rendezvous Mountain Trail (see Rendezvous Mountain Trail for description) also junctions at the cabin, but leads south between the Middle and South forks.

Granite Canyon Trail continues west up the North Fork. After about 0.8 miles from the cabin the trail junctions with the Open Canyon Trail (see Open Canyon Trail for description). This trail is a strenuous climb to Mount Hunt Divide and also accesses Mount Hunt, then drops down into Open Canyon to emerge at Phelps Lake.

Another 1.2 miles from the junction and the trail merges with the Teton Crest Trail (see Teton Crest-South for description). It is then a short 0.7 mile hike up to Marion Lake.

Marion Lake was named in honor of Marion Danford. She first ventured out West around 1915 as a guest of Struthers

Burt's Bar BC dude ranch. Burt, a Philadelphia writer, Princeton graduate and dude rancher, brought many of his wealthy Eastern friends to Jackson Hole. Granite Canyon was one of the favorite horseback excursions, where dudes nicknamed many of the features. (See Bar BC Ranch Trail for more detail on Bar BC Ranch.)

MARION LAKE.

Another Bar BC guest died in 1925 from a horse accident in this canyon. Fifteen-year-old Helen Mettler loved her summers in Grand Teton. In her journal from the previous summer she wrote, "God Bless Wyoming and Keep it Wild." This was her last entry for the summer before returning East. Her words have become a living tribute to the beauty, but untamed harshness of this wild country.

TETON VILLAGE TRAM TRAIL 🐴

Length: 7.2 miles, one way.
Elevation change: Trailhead at 6,311 feet (4,139-foot gain).
Trailhead: The trailhead begins at the Teton Village clock tower.

Teton Village Tram Trail provides one of the best views of Jackson Hole and the distant Gros Ventre Mountains. This trail during summer also provides a different perspective of the famous ski mountain. It also accesses the southern boundary of Grand Teton National Park.

The trail begins at the Teton Village clock tower and from there the trail heads north crossing the lower Teewinot ski slope to the beginning of a road that ascends the mountain.

Even though this is a popular summer hike it is not open for mountain biking. However, there are annual mountain bike hill climb competitions, but otherwise mountain bikes are excluded from the mountain.

From the base of the Teton Range the trail follows the ski mountain maintenance road, switchbacking up the hillside and providing views of the valley and of Teton Village below. About half way, or a little less, is the mountains half way hut. The Casper Restaurant is used by winter skiers as a warming and lunch house. Past the half way house the trail passes Crystal Springs and Casper Bowl chairlifts and crosses under the Bridger™ Gondola, constructed in 1997. And beyond that the trail crosses under the aerial tram and skirts the base of Thunder chairlift. From this vicinity are some of the best views of the village and of the ascending tram cars. Also at this point until late June, and sometimes later, this may be the highest point that can be reached by foot. Large snow patches and running water may hinder or halt hikers beyond Thunder.

The remaining trail continues south along Cheyenne Bowl, past Sublette chairlift, and up a ridge via switchbacks to the top of peak 10,450. At the wind blown summit are dwarfed and stunted Engelmann spruce. This is treeline, also known as krummholz, where normal shaped trees will not grow above this point. Because of fierce gale force winds, deep winter snow—over 33 feet annually—and high elevation, plants have either adapted or specialized to the harsh and short growing season. There are a number of colorful and unique flowers

AERIAL TRAM.

growing here, including purple silky phacelia, blue alpine forget-me-nots, golden old-man-of-the-mountain and purple saxifrage. There are usually wildflower identification displays at Corbet's Cabin, a small hut perched on the summit, as well as interesting fossils and geologic explanations.

The views from the top are spectacular, and there is even a mounted viewing binocular. To the east is the entire valley of Jackson Hole. To the south is Rendezvous Peak (10,927 feet) and to the distant west is the state of Idaho. To the north is Granite Creek drainage, Buck Mountain and even the tip of the Grand Teton.

Also on the top is a self-guiding nature trail and on the backside is the Rendezvous Mountain Trail (see Rendezvous Mountain Trail for description). This trail accesses either the Teton Crest Trail (see Teton Crest Trail for description) or the Granite Canyon drainage and trail. Once on the Granite Canyon Trail Marion Lake is at the head of the drainage or the hike down emerges at either the Granite Canyon parking area after 12.2 miles from the summit, or skirts the base of the mountain and returns to Teton Village.

PIKA.

Another way to descend from the summit is the aerial tramway. For hikers who walk up it is a free ride down. During most summers from late May until late September the tram operates every 15 minutes from 9 a.m. to 4 p.m. and the last tram leaves the summit at 4:30 p.m.. But before considering an actual excursion that involves the use and exact timing of the tram, please contact the Jackson Hole ski resort for the latest information.

RENDEZVOUS MOUNTAIN TRAIL

Length from top of aerial tramway to:

Middle Fork cutoff trail	3.4 miles, one way.
Marion Lake (spur trail)	7.8 miles, one way.
Granite Canyon patrol cabin	5.4 miles, one way.
Granite Canyon parking area	12.2 miles, one way.
Teton Village clock tower	13.1 miles, one way.

Elevation change: Trailhead at 10,450 feet (2,450-foot loss to Granite Canyon patrol cabin).

Trailhead: The summit of Rendezvous Mountain at the top of the aerial tramway, Teton Village.

The trailhead for Rendezvous Mountain Trail can be accessed two ways. But one is certainly more difficult than the other. Both begin at the Teton Village clock tower. One utilizes the tram/ski mountain maintenance road (see Teton Village Tram Trail for description), and is a vigorous 4,139-foot vertical, 7.2 mile climb. The other is a 15-minute ride (for a fee) up the aerial tram to the beginning of the trail.

The Rendezvous Mountain Trail is used primarily by tram riders who cruise down from the summit to Granite Canyon patrol cabin and out Granite Canyon to Teton Village. It is a popular all day summer hike with easy down hill terrain.

The trail also accesses the Teton Crest Trail (see Teton Crest Trail for description), and it also is the best route to Marion Lake, a small cirque lake at the head of Granite Canyon.

After leaving the tram dock the trail begins by heading southwest along a ridge. From there it drops into a small roundish amphitheater where snow lines the north facing slopes. This has been a popular glissading snowfield, but caution should be taken as numerous deaths have occurred here when out-of-control glissaders have plunged to their death onto the rocks at the bottom.

SERVICEBERRY.

UPPER GRANITE CANYON.

The trail continues over a ridge separating it from the South Fork of Granite Creek. By leaving the trail along this ridge and looking for rock outcroppings it is possible to find fossil rugose corals—or horn corals—and brachiopods—unequal valve, shelled marine animals—in the Ordovician to Permian age sedimentary rocks. From the ridge the trail again traverses another drainage. On the other side of the drainage is a junction to a cutoff trail that connects west to the Teton Crest Trail. This is the best and easiest route to Marion Lake.

The north trail heads down hill and junctions with the Granite Canyon Trail (see Granite Canyon Trail for description), leading to either the Granite Canyon parking area or skirting the base of Rendezvous Mountain and returning to Teton Village.

ALASKA BASIN

Length from Jenny Lake west shore boat dock to:

Hidden Falls	0.5 miles, one way.
Inspiration Point	1.0 miles, one way.
Cascade Canyon fork	4.6 miles, one way.
Avalanche Divide Trail junction	8.3 miles, one way.
Avalanche Divide spur trail	9.8 miles, one way.
Schoolroom Glacier	9.0 miles, one way.
Hurricane Pass	9.4 miles, one way.
Sunset Lake (Alaska Basin)	10.6 miles, one way.
Basin Lakes (Alaska Basin)	11.2 miles, one way.

Length from Whitegrass ranger station to:

Phelps Lake Overlook	0.9 miles, one way.
Phelps Lake trail junction	1.8 miles, one way.
Death Canyon patrol cabin	3.7 miles, one way.
Peak 10,552 trail junction	3.7 miles, one way.
Fox Creek Pass	8.6 miles, one way.
Basin Lakes (Alaska Basin)	13.9 miles, one way.

Length from Teton Canyon (Idaho) trailhead to:

Devil's Stairs	2.7 miles, one way.
Basin Lakes (Alaska Basin)	7.1 miles, one way.

Elevation change: Jenny Lake trailhead at 6,785 feet (2,815-foot gain to Basin Lakes, but a 3,605-foot gain to Hurricane Pass); Death Canyon Trailhead at 6,780 feet (2,820-foot gain to Basin Lakes, but a 2,280-foot gain to Fox Pass.); Teton Canyon trailhead at 6,955 feet (2,645-foot gain to Basin Lakes.)

Trailhead: Jenny Lake; Located at the southern shore of Jenny Lake at the developed parking area and using the boat launch to the west shore. Or an alternative route from the String Lake picnic area. Death Canyon; Starts at the Whitegrass ranger station parking area, just off the Moose-Wilson Road. The turnoff to Whitegrass is 3.1 miles south of Moose and it is another

MOOSE.

1.5 miles from the junction to the end of the road where the parking and trailhead are located. Teton Canyon; Located at the end of the Teton Canyon road, originating from Driggs, Idaho. Trailhead begins from the campground.

Alaska Basin is one of those rare utopian backcountry sites that has universal appeal. This open, high-elevation basin, spotted with little lakes is well-known for its summer wildflower display and peaceful serene subalpine setting. It is an isolated basin where the headwaters of Teton Creek form in a pocket just outside the boundary of Grand Teton National Park in Targhee National Forest.

The trail resides on the Teton Crest Trail (see Teton Crest Trail for description) and several approaches are available from either the east or west sides.

The most popular route originates at Jenny Lake and uses the Cascade Canyon Trail (see Schoolroom Glacier-South Fork Cascade Canyon Trail for description) to Hurricane Pass. From there the trail drops into Alaska Basin at the base of Battleship Mountain (10,679 feet).

The other route approaching from the east is via Death Canyon. This trail uses the Death Canyon Trail (see Death Canyon Trail and Static Peak Trail for description) and approaches the basin by either going over Static Peak or up Death Canyon and along the Death Canyon Shelf. Either route accesses the basin.

The easiest hiking approach is from the Idaho side. This route is accessible by driving up Teton Canyon by the way of Driggs. At the end of the road is a campground and the trailhead. From there the trail follows the South Fork of Teton Creek up into Alaska Basin.

Even though Alaska Basin is technically outside of the national park and on forest service land it receives high visitation. As a result National Park Service camping and backcountry regulations and restrictions apply to this region and permits are needed.

MOUNTAIN
TOWNSENDIA.

SNAKE RIVER DIKES 🚲 ⛷ 🐾

Length from Snake River bridge to:

Northeast dike	2.2 miles, one way.
Northwest dike	0.7 miles, one way.
Southwest dike	2.1 miles, one way.

Elevation change: Trailhead at 6,160 feet (no perceptual elevation change).

Trailhead: The trailheads begin at the Snake River bridge, 1.6 miles east of Wilson. This trailhead has three trail directions and the parking areas are located at each of the bridge abutments, except for the southeast dike. The parking area for the northwest dike is accessed by driving north through the traffic light. It is the first road heading east off the Moose-Wilson road.

The Snake River Dikes, like Cache Creek, are popular year-round hikes for Jackson locals. It is especially popular for walking the dog, or squeezing in a cross-country ski or a mountain bike trip on a hectic day.

Of the three accesses the northeast dike at Emily Stevens Park has been developed. The Bureau of Reclamation land-scaped the old Iron Rock quarry, creating a pond and a large parking area. From the parking area the trail is blocked off to vehicle traffic—except construction vehicles—and follows the dike north for about 2.2 miles to an orange gate. The Army Corps of Engineers dike wanders through cottonwood trees and occasional blue spruce across some private land at first and then Bureau of Land Management. It must be kept in mind that the levees cross private land and presently landowners have not objected to this use. But if it is abused or problems arise access could be denied, like the southeast dike.

WINTER ON THE
GRAND.

The levees were originally started in the late 1940s along the Snake River Ranch, opposite Teton Village. River bank erosion and flooded pasture lands prompted land owners to begin building dikes along the river. By the 1950s federal legislation was passed for a dike system administered by the Army Corps of Engineers with local and state government cooperation. Piece by piece the riverbank has been built up to a nearly continuous levee on each side of the river from the airport through South Park. The dike system is still an ongoing project with new additions and the rebuilding and restoration of existing dikes.

WESTERN OR
WANDERING GARTER
SNAKE.

One of the main problems and the need for dikes is that the valley floor is tipped downward toward the Tetons, a result of the Teton Fault and the resulting uplift of the mountains and a drop of the valley. From the river surface at the Snake River bridge to Wilson, a distance of only a mile and a half, there is a difference in elevation of nearly 8 feet. This means that during high water the area and all the homes built between the river and Wilson will have a tendency to flood. This is a natural occurrence. Water does flow downhill.

The trailhead on the northwest corner of the Snake River bridge is a primary boat launching access for river trips. There are even restrooms at the parking area. The dike is open to traffic, but it is a short 0.7 miles to the first gate. Beyond the gate is private property and they have restricted access across their land.

The last dike walk is the southwest levee. The parking is very limited with only a small turnout adjacent to the bridge abutment. This section of the dike also is open to vehicle traffic. The dike road crosses some private land and BLM land, but there are easements up to about 2.1 miles where a gate closes the road farther south. This road is especially popular as a ski trail since it is directly on the river bank. All roads, however, are unplowed during the winter and make excellent ski tours.

Hiking Gros Ventre

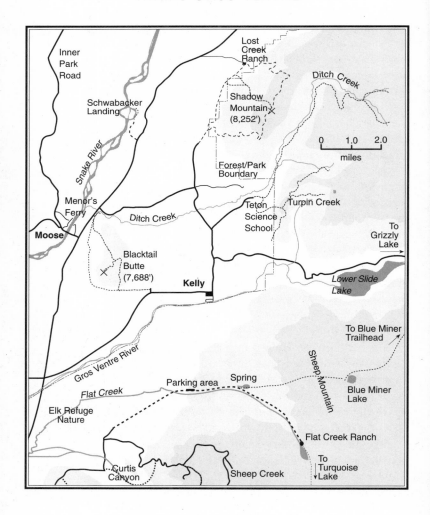

GROS VENTRE

This away-from-it-all region possesses the greatest contrast to the rest of Jackson Hole. Opposite the valley from the great Teton Range this drier, sedimentary mountain range does not have the Matterhorn-shaped peaks and glacial-carved canyons of its metamorphic neighbor.

Because of its lower elevation and southern exposed slopes, winter lessens its hold earlier and trails become snow free by May. But as summer progresses the region cures to a golden brown and becomes parched faster as a result.

This mountain range also attracts wintering wildlife including bighorn sheep, elk and mule deer. Pronghorn antelope migrate through the valleys from their wintering grounds near the Wind River Range to spend their summers in the valley. While blackbears prowl throughout the mountain range.

BLUE MINER LAKE IN THE GROS VENTRE RANGE.

Beyond the fauna is an incredible study of Gros Ventre flora. Wildflowers are more diverse than those found in the

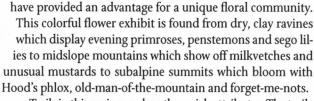

Teton Range. A variety of habitats, soil types and microclimates have provided an advantage for a unique floral community. This colorful flower exhibit is found from dry, clay ravines which display evening primroses, penstemons and sego lilies to midslope mountains which show off milkvetches and unusual mustards to subalpine summits which bloom with Hood's phlox, old-man-of-the-mountain and forget-me-nots.

BALD EAGLE.

Trails in this region explore these rich attributes. The trails reach into canyons via stream courses, over mountain summits via their bellies or to cirque lakes by the way of dry, ancient morainal ridges.

OSPREY.

SHADOW MOUNTAIN TRAIL 🚲 🎿 🥾

Length from the base of Shadow Mountain to:

Shadow Mountain summit	3.7 miles, one way.
Mid-mountain bike trail	3.8 miles, one way.
Lost Creek Ranch	7.6 miles, one way.
Shadow Mountain bike loop	6.8 miles, loop.
Shadow Mountain road loop	9.8 miles, loop.

Elevation change: Trailhead at 6,810 feet (1,442-foot gain).
Trailhead: Located at the base of Shadow Mountain on the park/forest service boundary. The trailhead is 5.8 miles east of Antelope Flats junction on U.S. highway 89-187. The Antelope Flats road has a four-way junction, called mailbox junction (no mailboxes, however, exist anymore), and the Shadow Mountain road heads north. Just before the end of the pavement the dirt Shadow Mountain road junctions and continues north to the base of the mountain.

Shadow Mountain has long been known for its scenic four-wheel drive route, but since the early 1990s it has become one of the top mountain bike excursions in the region. It also is well-known for its cross-country skiing, but less so for its hiking advantages. One of the best aspects of Shadow Mountain is the incredible view. It has the best and unparalleled vantage points of the entire Teton Range.

Shadow Mountain sits in the Teton National Forest, just outside of the park boundary. The mountain can be approached from either the south, via Antelope Flats, or from the north, via Lost Creek Ranch. Either approach provides a number of loops, side trips or routes.

The southern approach, however, is the most popular access. Just as the pavement ends, and before the trailhead, is a large home. This new home, built in the mid 1990s, was built on the site of artist Conrad Schwiering's home. Schwiering was Wyoming's premier, impressionist landscape painter. He and his wife, Mary Ethel, both died in 1986, and they are buried on the hillside north of the new house.

Just as the road begins to climb the steep mountain is the trailhead and parking. (During winter the trailhead is located at the beginning of the dirt road but this can be pushed back to mailbox junction in heavy snow years.) From the base it is a steep ascent. This mountain is especially popular for telemark and cross-country skiing. Usually a ski track follows the road to the top and a number of powder, open or treed, slopes are available for the descent. This area of the mountain also shows signs of the 1988 Shadow Mountain forest fire. Even large, somewhat fire resistant Douglas firs burned. But the area also shows the typical effects of forest fire, where a mosaic of burned and unburned patches lie side by side.

During the summer the road to the summit, also called Antelope Peak (8,252 feet), wanders north along the ridge and then descends to Lost Creek Ranch. From there it is possible to return to the outer park road (U.S. highway 89-187), opposite Snake River Overlook. Or the road loops back and follows the base of the mountain and returns to the trailhead. This road provides a great mountain bike loop and also can be hiked, but expect an occasional vehicle chugging its way up.

For mountain bikers or hikers there is an alternative route. At the summit is a trail that descends the center of the mountain. The trail is very steep and rough in some places, but wanders through the coniferous and aspen forest. About half way the trail splits. Either trail ends in a gully and merges with the road running along the base of the mountain.

DITCH CREEK TRAIL 🔺 🚲 ⛷ 🐕

Length from trailhead to:

End of logging road	5.4 miles, one way.
Lower Slide Lake	13.9 miles, one way.

Elevation change: Trailhead at 7,063 feet (1,187-foot gain to the end of the logging road).

Trailhead: The trail is located behind the Teton Science School, just north of Kelly. The Forest Service access road curves behind the school and enters the mouth of the canyon. The old logging road is blocked off and the trail begins at that point.

There are few trails that lead into and explore the front range of the Gros Ventre Mountains. Ditch Creek is one of the few. Since the road is outside of Grand Teton National Park it can be hiked, mountain biked or cross-country skied with the dog.

Ditch Creek, so named because its waters were diverted by ditches to irrigate hay fields and pasture land on Antelope Flats, flows past the Teton Science School. The school was once the second Elbo dude ranch. It was purchased by the National Park Service and by the mid 1970s the school moved into the old ranch buildings. The school functions primarily as a science and natural history education center for junior high-aged students where they spend a week at the facilities studying everything from animal tracks to zoology.

The school also houses the Olaus Murie collection. Murie was one of the leading biologists for the Biological Survey—forerunner to the U.S. Fish and Wildlife Service. He also is the author of the Peterson field guide book, *A Field Guide to Animal Tracks.* He extensively collected, illustrated and wrote about Alaska before moving to Jackson Hole in 1927 to study elk. The collection includes specimens of most Western birds and mammals, their scat, impressions of their tracks and hundreds of Murie's field drawings and watercolors. The museum, however, is not open to the public and a great educational resource is not accessible.

At the park/forest boundary is a cluster of small cabins, a private ranch, and just beyond is the trailhead. The trail wanders up Ditch Creek, past old beaver ponds and willow marshes. The mountain to the west is the backside of Shadow Mountain (see Shadow Mountain Trail for description). This old logging and oil exploration road continues up Ditch Creek until it dead ends at an oil test well.

Just around the bend before the road dead ends a trail heads directly down slope to Ditch Creek and about a mile upstream the trail and creek forks. The North Fork Ditch Creek trail leads into the remote Mount Leidy highlands.

The other trail, Middle Fork Ditch Creek, heads south and crosses over a divide into the Horsetail Creek drainage. The trail follows this drainage and emerges at the Gros Ventre road at Lower Slide Lake.

COYOTE.

TURPIN CREEK TRAIL 🎿 🐕

Length from Elbo Ranch (Teton Science School) trailhead to:

Turpin Creek Pass	1.6 miles, one way.
Upper Turpin Creek spur trail	3.0 miles, one way.
Lower Turpin Creek	2.9 miles, one way.
Gros Ventre River Ranch	4.1 miles, one way.

Elevation change: Trailhead at 7,075 feet (1,082-foot gain to peak in Upper Turpin Creek and 503-foot gain to peak in Lower Turpin Creek).

BRITTLE CACTUS.

Trailhead: The trailhead is located behind the Teton Science School, just north of Kelly. The Forest Service access road curves behind the school for about a half mile. On the south side of the road is a pull out and the beginning of the trail.

Turpin Creek Trail, perched on the eastern boundary of the park and forest, wanders in the foothills at the base of the

Gros Ventre Mountains. The trail has been a popular outing for residents and students of Teton Science School for winter ski excursions or spring wildflower trips.

In spring some of the first flowers to emerge in the valley are found on these south facing slopes. Sagebrush buttercups are some of the first to appear, with milkvetches, evening primrose and prickly pear cactus following into summer.

The trail begins in an aspen and Douglas fir stand and heads south over a saddle east of a small knoll. The knoll (7,332 feet) can be easily climbed and provides a wonderful view of Ditch Creek drainage and the Science School compound.

From the saddle the trail makes a sharp directional change to the east up a ravine to another saddle which drops into Turpin Creek drainage, but the trail does not drop into the drainage. At the saddle the faint trail splits. The north trail follows the ridge line for about a mile and a half to an unnamed peak (8,157 feet) near the head of Turpin Creek.

The south trail continues along the ridge to another unnamed point (7,578 feet). This point provides views toward Antelope Flats and Blacktail Butte. It is possible to drop into

SHEEP MOUNTAIN, ALSO KNOWN AS SLEEPING INDIAN.

Turpin Creek or continue following the ridge. Both emerge onto the Gros Ventre road near Gros Ventre River Ranch.

The foothills between Ditch Creek and the Gros Ventre River is a fascinating country. In the spring the southern exposures are the first to loose their snow and provide hikers with dirt footing. Game trails, established by bighorn sheep, antelope, deer and elk, crisscross the area and provide a maze of exploratory trails. Just keep a sense of location and direction while exploring.

SHEEP MOUNTAIN 🐎
(Sleeping Indian)

Length: 3.0 miles, one way.
Elevation change: Trailhead at 7,185 feet (3,625-foot gain).
Trailhead: Located east of the National Elk Refuge on the Flat Creek road. A parking area is 9.4 miles northeast of Jackson at the mouth of Flat Creek Canyon. Parking is available here since the road into Flat Creek Ranch is the roughest in the valley. But it is possible, with high clearance vehicles, to continue 1.3 miles to the base of Sheep Mountain and the trailhead.

Sheep Mountain, or more popularly known as Sleeping Indian for its west profile, is a dry but exciting hike to a premier peak of the Gros Ventre Mountains. From the belly of the Sleeping Indian it is possible to view the length of the Teton Range and the entire valley of Jackson Hole.

To reach the trailhead the Flat Creek Ranch Trail (see Flat Creek Ranch Trail for description) utilizes the same approach. It is best to park at the parking area at the boundary of the refuge and forest service, at the mouth of Flat Creek Canyon. Past that point the road becomes extremely rough and even the additional 1.3 miles to the trailhead can be impassable for low clearance cars, or any vehicle if the road is muddy after a recent rain.

The trailhead, however, can be found at the base of Sheep Mountain. It is distinguishable by a small parking area located at a sharp bend in the main road that heads south and steeply up a hill. At the parking area is a spring, basically a moist seep. This spring becomes prominent during July through September when the surrounding grasses have cured brown and the spring shows up as a lush green point in the landscape.

From the spring it is a bushwhack to the belly of Sheep Mountain. The unmarked trail heads east and up slope. There is no designated trail, but by using route finding sense follow the ridge east across open slope. At about 8,200 feet the route and ridge becomes coniferous tree covered. From there to the belly is through trees and ravines. Pick the best route through these to the open, exposed belly of Sleeping Indian. The belly

OLD-MAN-OF-THE-MOUNTAIN.

is a gently rounded mountain top. It is a wind blown subalpine summit and during July to mid August the mountain top is dotted with brilliant colors of subalpine wildflowers, including milkvetches, Hood's phlox, old-man-of-the-mountain and unusual mustards.

Sleeping Indian became nationally known in August 1996 when an Air Force cargo plane carrying President Clinton's

Secret Service gear crashed into the mountain. The pilot, a woman Air Force captain, of the C-1 cargo plane while making a night departure from Jackson Hole airport did not follow flight procedures and crashed into the belly of Sleeping Indian. A large fireball was seen by valley residents. Nine were killed in

STICKY GERANIUM.   the crash, including one Secret Service agent, and all crew members of the plane. All debris of the crash was immediately removed and no evidence remains of the "incident".

From the rounded belly of the summit are incredible views of the valley and from there several adventurous routes are possible. To the south it is possible to continue up the belly of the Indian to the folded hands on the chest. This point is at 11,239 feet and the summit of Sheep Mountain. Beyond this point is sheer cliffs to the south.

At the belly again, it also is possible to return north to the Gros Ventre road via the legs of the Sleeping Indian. This is another possible route, but a longer one. The route leads along the barren windswept ridge northward to the Gros Ventre Slide. Just before the slide the route enters trees, make sure the route to the east of the slide is followed. This will emerge at the Gros Ventre dam and the bridge to the Gros Ventre Road.

At the belly again another route is possible. This trail begins along the eastern edge of the belly. A large cirque containing Blue Miner Lake has steep, sheer cliffs, by circumnavigating this along the northern edge the Blue Miner Trail (see Blue

Miner Trail for description) becomes visible. This route leads
to the Gros Ventre road and emerges at the Hansen Ranch at
the concrete bridge on the river.

GRIZZLY LAKE TRAIL ▲ 🚲 🐎

10/00 Norm TH to TH

Length from Red Hills campground trailhead to:

Blue Miner Lake Trail junction	1.3 miles, one way.
Grizzly Lake	3.2 miles, one way.

Lots of up + down several ridges + wade river to reach w. TH.

Elevation change: Trailhead at 7,011 feet (173-foot gain to Grizzly Lake, but a 602-foot gain over the highest foothill).
Trailhead: The trailhead is located by driving past Kelly and
eastward along the Gros Ventre road past Lower Slide Lake. At
the end of the pavement it is about 3.5 miles to the trailhead. It
is located just past the Gros Ventre River concrete bridge and
just before the turnoff to Red Hills campground. On the south
side of the road is an unmarked parking area next to a small
knoll and a fence.

See Recreation Map GTNP (waterproof)

Grizzly Lake Trail is a short hike to a small lake in the foothills of the Gros Ventre Mountains. Grizzly Lake has been a
popular trail for exercising and swimming the dog.

The first section of this trail utilizes the Blue Miner Lake
Trail (see Blue Miner Lake Trail for description). The trailhead
is located across from the Red Hills campground and begins at
the base of a small knoll. The trail circumnavigates the Hansen
Ranch, following the eastern and southern perimeter of the
fence line. But there is another longer approach that utilizes the Crystal Creek Trail and junctions with this trail
near the corner of the Hansen Ranch.

On the other side of West Miner Creek the trail junctions
at the base of a ridge leading to Blue Miner Lake. Just past the
ridge the trail reaches its apex and the trail slowly drops into
the basin of Grizzly Lake.

Grizzly Lake is an old kettle formed by glacial ice. Ice was
buried during the last glacial retreat nearly 10,000 years ago.
Afterward the ice slowly melted leaving a depression. Runoff

PRONGHORN.

water now fills the depression, but the lake level fluctuates with wet and dry seasons.

It is possible to return to the Gros Ventre road directly across the river. There is an old horse trail that fords the Gros Ventre River and intersects the road near the pavements end. This route, however, is very treacherous since the Gros Ventre River is a major tributary of the Snake River. It should not be attempted in late spring or early summer during high runoff. Even during late summer this is an extremely dangerous undertaking.

BLUE MINER LAKE TRAIL

Length from Red Hills campground trailhead to:

Grizzly Lake Trail junction	1.3 miles, one way.
Blue Miner Lake	6.2 miles, one way.
Sheep Mountain	7.3 miles, one way.

Elevation change: Trailhead at 7,011 feet (2,391-foot gain to Blue Miner Lake or 3,799-foot gain to the belly of Sheep Mountain). Trailhead: The trailhead is located north of Kelly and east on the Gros Ventre road past Lower Slide Lake. At the end of the pavement it is about 3.5 miles to the trailhead. It is located just past the Gros Ventre River concrete bridge and just before the turnoff to Red Hills campground. On the south side of the road is an unmarked parking area next to a small knoll and a fence.

ALPINE MILKVETCH.

Blue Miner Lake is an unusual hike in that it begins in dry, nearly desert conditions along the Gros Ventre River and leads to a mountain lake or up the back of Sheep Mountain—also known as Sleeping Indian—to the windswept summit.

The trailhead begins near the Gros Ventre River bridge at the Hansen Ranch. Until the 1980s it was possible to start hiking from the bridge southward through the ranch. But a fence was put up around the property and now the fence line must be circumvented.

About 0.4 of a mile east of the concrete bridge is a small knoll and at the base is a small parking area. The trail follows the straight perimeter of the fence first south, then west. Once on the other side of the ranch the trail begins its climb up the morainal ridge of an old glacier. At the base of this ridge is the junction to Grizzly Lake (see Grizzly Lake Trail for description). For most of the hike the trail climbs this ridge.

Views from the ridge are fantastic. To the north are the colorful Red Hills, composed of red soil tinted by iron oxides. To the west are glimpses of the Teton Range and to the east, the upper Gros Ventre River valley. To the south is West Miner Creek drainage.

At a small point, or leveling of the ridge trail, is a small somewhat faint trail that heads down into the drainage. It is steep and not maintained, since it is not an official trail. It does, however, lead to the boulder ridden shore of Blue Miner Lake. The lake sits in a steep, rocky cirque. Because of the cliffs this spur trail ends at the lake.

BLUE MINER LAKE.

The ridge trail continues climbing and provides excellent views down into the small, blue waters of the lake. The lake is surrounded in a horseshoe shape by steep rocky walls. The trail climbs above the lake along the edge of the cirque to the barren windswept summit of Sheep Mountain (see Sheep Mountain Trail for description). This is the belly of what is popularly known as Sleeping Indian. From the summit a bushwhack trail leads down the west face of Sheep Mountain into Flat Creek.

FLAT CREEK RANCH TRAIL 🚲 🐎

Length: 5.4 miles, one way.
Elevation change: Trailhead at 6,829 feet (637-foot gain).
Trailhead: Located east of the National Elk Refuge on the Flat Creek Road. The parking area is 9.4 miles from Jackson at the mouth of Flat Creek Canyon. At the beginning of the canyon is a large parking area, just inside the national forest boundary.

This small Shangri-la valley is so close to Jackson, but yet so remote that it remains an isolated gem.

To access Flat Creek it is necessary to drive to east Jackson and north on the elk refuge road to connect with the Flat Creek road. At the refuge/forest service boundary is a large parking area. It is best to park here because the remaining road is the roughest stretch of road in Jackson Hole.

The road from the parking area can either be hiked, horsebacked or mountain biked. Mountain bikes are highly recommended on this rough two track. The old road is very rocky, with mud holes, creek crossings and steep inclines. The road has claimed numerous oil pans and axils, and for that reason personal vehicles are discouraged.

The first section of road accesses Sheep Mountain, alias Sleeping Indian (see Sheep Mountain Trail for description). The trailhead is located at a small parking area and natural spring at the first sharp bend and incline in the road.

From the spring, characterized by its greenness and lush

FLAT CREEK RANCH.

growth compared to its surroundings, the old road follows between the base of Sheep Mountain and parallels Flat Creek. As the road worsens the scenic value increases.

This famous ranch was once owned by Eleanor "Cissy" Patterson, the granddaughter of Joseph Medill, owner of the Chicago Tribune. Cissy had a pampered and sheltered childhood. She rebelled as a debutante and travelled through Europe, meeting nobility, including a Polish Ukraine, Count Josef Gizyki, whom she married. After her marriage she returned with the Count to his castle, which actually turned out to be a dilapidated house still containing the belongings of his last mistress. At that time he admitted he married her only for her money. After five years of an abusive, tumultuous marriage, Cissy escaped in the middle of the night with her daughter Felicia.

The Count in retaliation kidnapped their daughter and hid her in a convent deep in the Polish Ukraine. President William Taft had to be called upon to help return the child and terminate their marriage.

The marriage changed Cissy and she hardened. Afterward she immersed herself in work, becoming editor of the Washington *Times-Herald*, a struggling newspaper in 1930. She later became owner-editor of the thriving newspaper.

Her trips to Wyoming, beginning in 1916, were the only fond memories she had. She returned frequently and was eventually able to purchase the 140 acre Flat Creek Ranch from "Cal" Carrington for $5,000. After the sale Cal remained as foreman. Cissy, with her flamboyant style, then began bringing her numerous Eastern society friends to Jackson Hole.

Meanwhile Cissy had a falling out with her 18-year-old daughter Felicia and on Cissy's death in 1948 she left the property to her cousin Josephine Patterson Reese (Albright). Josephine, a wild spirit in her own right, was an early mail pilot and like her aunt, also immersed in the newspaper business. Josephine, however, was not interested in living at the ranch but leased it out. In 1986 Josephine donated the ranch to the Land Trust with a stipulation that on her death, which occurred in January 1996, her children would have the option to purchase the ranch from the Land Trust, but with preservation rights intact. One son, Joe, did purchase the ranch, his ex-wife Madeleine Albright, was United Nations ambassador and later became secretary of state.

The ranch is now off limits to hikers and bikers, but there is a trail that skirts the northern and eastern boundary of the property. This trail begins at the Flat Creek Ranch gate and runs along the hillside of Sheep Mountain. From the trail are great views of the man-enlarged lake and the cabins sited at the outlet. The trail again merges with Flat Creek and does continue up the Flat Creek drainage, or to a cutoff trail crossing over into the Granite Creek drainage. Both routes eventually lead to Turquoise Lake (see Turquoise Lake for description).

KINNIKINNICK.

Hiking Jackson

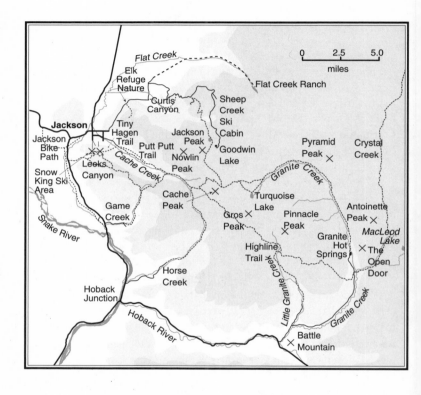

JACKSON

The town site of Jackson sits in a pocket at the southern end of Jackson Hole. The expansive elk refuge begins on its northern edge, Snow King Mountain lies to the south, and the mouth of Cache Creek opens toward town from the east.

Within this hub of activity are numerous of trails that radiate from here. Mountain biking, horse riding, skiing or hiking trails climb, traverse, meander or cross into the surrounding region.

Numerous trails, especially bike paths and walk-the-dog trails, originate from Jackson. These make it very convenient for Jackson residents to step onto a trail and quickly enter into another world.

This world, however, has transgressed from the days when early trappers were here. In the 1820s to 1840s the West was relatively active with John Jacob Astor's American fur trappers. They were seeking fur bearing animals, especially beaver used in the making of beaver felt hats—top hats of European fashion for the social elite.

JACKSON DURING THE 1960S FROM THE TOP OF SNOW KING.

One trapper in particular, David Jackson, became fond of this valley and soon other trappers began referring to it as Jackson's Hole. Hole was a trapper term for a valley in which there was no visible means of escape. In other words it was surrounded by mountains.

At that time elk wandered their traditional migration from Yellowstone to what is now the southern boundary of Wyoming. This migration was almost a constant movement of animals from northern summer grounds to southern wintering grounds. By the time the town of Jackson was established, farmers set up their operations in the fertile valley bottoms and in the direct migration route of elk. The vast number of elk conflicted with farms and a fence was placed across Jackson in the late nineteenth century to impede their southward movement. As a result elk now spend their winter on land set aside for them on the National Elk Refuge.

ELK REFUGE NATURE TRAIL
Length: 2.5 miles, one way.
Elevation change: Trailhead at 6,310 feet (2,466-foot gain).
Trailhead: Located across from Miller's Butte on the National Elk Refuge, 2.3 miles north of Jackson on the elk refuge road.

The Elk Refuge Nature Trail is one of the few trails near town and the only trail that begins in the National Elk Refuge. Hiking is prohibited in the elk refuge, but this trail actually accesses the corner of Teton National Forest in less than a tenth of a mile.

This trail was originally a forest access trail, especially for hunters on horseback. It was renamed and marked in the early 1990s as a nature trail. The trail rises steeply via a series of switchbacks to a mid-elevation, unnamed peak overlooking Jackson, Miller's Butte, the elk refuge and beyond to the Tetons.

This mountain and nearby Miller's Butte often harbor mountain lions. They are very elusive, but occasionally are seen in the vicinity.

From the mountain intermittent game trails radiate in all directions, and from there it is difficult to choose a trail. It is possible, however, to bushwhack south into Woods Canyon and enter Cache Creek from that point.

CURTIS CANYON TRAIL

Length: 1.6 miles, one way.
Elevation change: Trailhead at 7,050 feet (550-foot gain).
Trailhead: Located at the Curtis Canyon campground, on the eastern edge of the National Elk Refuge. The start of the trail begins at the end of the campground loop.

WATER HEMLOCK.

This is a little-known trail out of the Curtis Canyon campground and is used primarily by campers staying there. But the trail provides a wonderful excursion to a viewpoint overlooking the refuge and a hike into a cool narrow canyon.

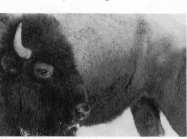

BISON.

At the end of the campground loop a trail leads out into a meadow and along a two track. This is the beginning of the Curtis Canyon Trail. Just at the start is a faint trail leading west up to a ridge. This is a good side trip to a vantage point overlooking the National Elk Refuge and he Teton Range.

The two track, the remnants of an old road, heads through the meadow and down the canyon past an old abandoned tractor, then into the trees and along North Twin Creek. Along the narrow canyon is a small diversion pond used by Twin Creek Ranch as the source for their domestic water. Screens filter out floating debris, such as leaves and needles. The spring water is then piped down through a sand filter before gravity delivers it to the residents below. This was a common and very efficient means of a clean water source for early residents in Jackson Hole. Now, however, most new homes either obtain their water from a domestic water supply or by means of a drilled well.

The trail continues through a narrow constriction and emerges at the mouth of the canyon at Twin Creek Ranch. But, because this is private property and the trail merges with a private road crossing a retired judge's property there is no trespassing. Thus there is no connection with the elk refuge road, and the only available route is to return up the canyon to the campground.

This trail would be an excellent mountain bike trail, if it were not for the short stretch—a couple hundred feet—of private property separating it from the elk refuge. But respect private property and return to the trailhead, even if it does mean an uphill trudge.

GOODWIN LAKE TRAIL 🐾

Length: 3.0 miles, one way.
Elevation change: Trailhead at 8,180 feet (1,320-foot gain).
Trailhead: The trailhead is reached by driving through the National Elk Refuge to Curtis Canyon. This stretch of road from the town of Jackson to the turnoff of the Goodwin Lake road is 9.0 miles (1.2 miles past the Curtis Canyon campground). The Goodwin Lake road is another 1.2 miles to its terminus and the graveled parking area at the trailhead.

LIMBER PINE.

Goodwin Lake is a popular trail in the Bridger-Teton National Forest. The trail leads to this small subalpine lake at the base of Jackson Peak (10,741 feet). The trailhead was relocated in 1995 and it added an extra mile to the route. But the new access provides a more scenic route with fewer switchbacks.

During summer the trail leads up slope through wild-flower carpeted meadows filled with three-veined sunflowers, fireweed, sticky geranium, Engelmann aster, showy green gentian, sandwort and Indian paintbrush. The meadows are fringed with quaking aspen and Douglas fir. As the trail ascends the ridge these trees give way to subalpine fir, Engelmann spruce and limber pine.

For most of the hike to Goodwin Lake the trail ascends and then follows along the edge of a knifelike ridge. This ridge is really a lateral glacial moraine. Glacial ice, originating at Goodwin Lake, flowed down the valley to the east along what is now Sheep Creek. As the ice receded about 12,000 to 15,000 years ago, rock and other glacial debris was deposited along

its flank leaving a natural berm about 200-400 feet high. It is composed of unconsolidated glacial till consisting of everything from fine silts, sands, gravels to large boulders.

GOODWIN LAKE.

Shortly before Goodwin Lake the trail has been diverted across the lake's outlet. This junction leads to the eastern shore of the lake and the trail continues onward to Turquoise Lake (see Turquoise Lake Trail for description). This side of the lake is heavily forested with a grassy shoreline. The better, but cooler, campsites are located here.

The western shore is at the base of a scree slope leading to Jackson Peak—the peak's summit is not visible from the lake. The best aspect of this shore is the large polished rock outcropping that projects into the lake. It is a popular lounging rock for picnicking, sunbathing or as a diving platform for those brave enough to submerse themselves into the frigid water of the lake.

Goodwin Lake sits in a glacial cirque—or bowl, where the ancient glacier formed. As the river of ice flowed it pulled rock from the headwall, carrying it by gravity and later depositing it along the side or toe of the glacier. Along its journey some of this suspended debris was scraped and ground along the bottom of the glacier against bedrock, polishing and streamlining any natural bedrock feature. Glacial grooves and polished granite are visible on some of these features.

The trail does continue from Goodwin Lake. One possible side trip is a scramble up to the summit of Jackson Peak. There is a partial trail leading to the scree slope, but the trail becomes lost from there and route finding becomes necessary. There also is a false summit, but once that has been climbed the true summit can be reached by continuing down the ridge. The summit is 1,241 feet above Goodwin Lake.

Another popular destination, especially for winter skiing, is the Goodwin Lake ski cabin. It is a little over a half mile from the lake. It was built in 1953 by local and Idaho Falls skiers for backcountry use and as an emergency winter shelter. It has been maintained by donated help and has been available to the public. In the late 1980s the Forest Service wanted to tear down the cabin, but local outcry prevented it from being razed. However, in retaliation the Forest Service closed the Curtis Canyon-Goodwin Lake access to skiers, essentially isolating the cabin for winter use. Now the only access is by skiing up Cache Creek by a circuitous route or a very long trip up Granite Creek. If this closure continues over time the cabin will be forgotten and will eventually and silently be eliminated.

TURQUOISE LAKE TRAIL ▲ 🐎

Length from Cache Creek parking area to:

Tiny Hagen Trail	0.0 miles, one way.
Putt Putt Trail junction	2.2 miles, one way.
Game Creek Trail junction	3.8 miles, one way.
Horse Creek Trail junction	5.5 miles, one way.
Granite Highline trail junction	6.2 miles, one way.
Goodwin Lake trail junction	9.1 miles, one way.
Flat Creek Trail junction	9.2 miles, one way.
Turquoise Lake	11.5 miles, one way.

Elevation change: Trailhead at 6,444 feet (3,016-foot gain to Turquoise Lake, but a 3,696-foot gain to Gros Ventre pass).

Trailhead: Located at the mouth of Cache Creek Canyon on the east edge of the town of Jackson. Cache Creek Drive is located at the end of Redmond Street and Cache Creek Drive enters the canyon. Just after the pavement ends is a large parking area by the creek. The trail begins behind the barricade.

One of the longer trails in Jackson Hole leads to this backcountry lake in the remote interior of the Teton National Forest. The lake is perched at the base of the Gros Ventre Range.

Even for its remoteness it has a number of accesses including Goodwin Lake, Flat Creek Ranch and Granite Creek (see respective trails for description). But one of the easiest is through Cache Creek canyon. Using this route is primarily a straight shot up the canyon over the divide at its head, past Cache Peak, through the upper Gros Ventre Range to Turquoise Lake.

The first section of trail utilizes the Cache Creek Trail (see Cache Creek Trail for description). This trail reaches the upper recesses of the drainage where the trail junctions with the North Fork Trail. At this junction the Turquoise Lake trail heads directly east and up, out of the Cache Creek drainage. Halfway up slope, before the trail begins switchbacks, the trail junctions again. This time with the Granite Highline Trail.

TWO SIMILAR BIRDS—
THE GRAY JAY, TOP,
IS A COMMON
CAMPGROUND PEST,
WHILE THE CLARK'S
NUTCRACKER,
BOTTOM, IS A NOISY
BIRD FOUND NEAR
TREELINE.

The trail continues climbing via switchbacks, but circum-navigates Cache Peak (10,304 feet) to the south. The trail then traverses the divide of Flat Creek and passes through a low saddle in the Gros Ventre Range at about 10,140 feet. Near this point are two more trail junctions only 0.1 mile apart. These lead to either Goodwin Lake or a spur trail of Granite Creek. From the pass it is downhill to Turquoise Lake at 9,460 feet elevation.

This upper plateau region is generally snow covered until late June to mid July, and even the lake is usually ice covered until then. Wind blown and twisted limber pines and barren windswept subalpine, rocky outcroppings testify to the extreme nature of this terrain. But it is a fascinating and wild region of the Gros Ventre.

From Turquoise Lake the trail does continue down the

Granite Creek drainage and emerges at Granite Creek Hot Springs (see Granite Creek Trail for description), approximately 11.0 miles away.

CACHE CREEK TRAIL 🔺 🚲 ⛷ 🐎

Length from Cache Creek parking area to:

Tiny Hagen Trail	0.0 miles, one way.
Putt Putt Trail junction	2.2 miles, one way.
Game Creek Trail junction	3.8 miles, one way.
Cache Pass	6.2 miles, one way.

Elevation change: Trailhead at 6,444 feet (2,542-foot gain).

Trailhead: Located at the mouth of Cache Creek Canyon on the

TRUMPETER SWAN CYGNET.

east edge of the town of Jackson. At the end of Cache Creek Drive, just after the pavement ends is a large parking area by the creek. The trail begins behind the barricade.

Cache Creek Trail is easily accessible by Jackson town residents, and it is a popular hiking, biking and skiing trail for those with limited time or need a quick break. It also is one of the few areas for walking the dog and many regulars walk their dogs on a daily basis. For its convenient location, Cache Creek is an exciting canyon for all-season activities leading to jump off points to a number of divergent trails.

This is truly a winter and summer trail. During summer the trail is lined with wildflowers, including sticky geranium, lodgepole lupine, arrowleaf balsamroot and Indian paintbrush. Winter along the trail is another world. Because of the lower angle of the winter sun the canyon is darker, colder and as a result the trail freezes and ices up, providing a solid, but slick, route up the canyon. The south facing slope, however, is draped in smooth skiable snow.

Cache Creek Trail is actually a two track that follows the

creek. The old road fizzles out at a defunct mine at Noker Mine draw and becomes a path from that point.

Cache Creek is certainly a utilitarian trail since it provides access to a number of other trails and locales, including the popular Putt Putt Trail (see Putt Putt Trail for description) and the Game Creek Trail (see Game Creek Trail for description). From these two junctions the trail continues climbing to the head of Cache Creek drainage and the base of Cache Peak (10,304 feet), a pyramid-shaped peak looming east up the canyon, to a pass which connects to Granite Canyon (see Granite Canyon Trail for description).

PUTT PUTT TRAIL

Length: 4.5 mile, loop.
Elevation change: Trailhead at 6,444 feet (506-foot gain).
Trailhead: Located at the mouth of Cache Creek Canyon on the southeastern edge of the town of Jackson. At the end of Cache Creek Drive, just after the pavement ends is a large parking area by the creek. The trail begins behind the barricade.

The Putt Putt Trail is a favorite mountain bike path among locals, especially those living in town as an after work excursion. It is a fun bicycle loop and known for its roller-coaster downhill ride.

The trail begins at the Cache Creek parking area and follows the old road up the canyon and along the creek. This is the same trail as the Cache Creek Trail (see Cache Creek Trail for description), but junctions after about 2.2 miles. The junction is usually unmarked, but distinguished by a sharp juncture on the north side of the road. The trail parallels the Cache Creek Trail back down the canyon along the base of the Gros Ventre Mountains. The trail is up and down dropping into each ravine and climbing each foothill, producing the down hill, roller coaster ride.

CHOKECHERRY.

The trail also wanders among aspen stands and lodgepole pines and in early summer brilliant patches of wildflowers, before looping back to the Cache Creek road, just below the parking area.

CACHE-GAME CREEK TRAIL 🚲 ⛷ 🐎

Length from Cache Creek parking area to:

Tiny Hagen Trail	0.0 miles, one way.
Putt Putt Trail junction	2.2 miles, one way.
Game Creek Trail junction	3.8 miles, one way.
Game Creek pass	5.0 miles, one way.
Game Creek bridge	9.0 miles, one way.
U.S highway 89	10.2 miles, one way.
New Post Office	16.5 miles, one way.
Return to Cache Creek	19.8 mile, loop.

Elevation change: Trailhead at 6,444 feet (966-foot gain to Cache-Game Creek pass, or 451-foot loss to the end of Game Creek at highway 89).

Trailhead: Located at the mouth of Cache Creek Canyon on the southeastern edge of the town of Jackson. At the end of Cache Creek Drive, just after the pavement ends is a large parking area by the creek. The trail begins behind the barricade.

Cache-Game Creek Trail is one of the more popular mountain bike excursions in the valley. It is easily accessed from Jackson and provides a good long loop of interesting and varied terrain.

Beginning at the Cache-Creek parking area the trail utilizes the Cache Creek Trail (see Cache Creek Trail for description) for the first 3.8 mile section. At the junction with Game Creek Trail the trail dips into the creek bottom and crosses the creek and then begins the up hill climb by traversing to the pass separating the two drainages. From the pass it is all down hill through Game Creek to U.S. highway 89. For the first section it is a steep trail, but once into the creek bottom, marked by a fording, it leisurely follows an old two track along the creek. The old road then merges with the paved Game Creek Road at the culvert, and from there it is about a mile to the highway.

DESERT PARSLEY.

At the highway it is a 9.6 mile return to Cache Creek trailhead. Until the late 1990s it was a dangerous bike ride on the highway back to town. But beginning in 1996 construction began for a bike path that wanders south of town through South Park, Rafter J and Melody Ranch. By 1998 it connected to the mouth of Game Creek. Eventually the path will connect to Hoback junction.

RABBITBRUSH.

By staying on the bike path it provides a safe and a more interesting return route, but the path ends in town at the new post office. From there it is necessary to utilize Snow King Avenue and Cache Creek Drive to return to the trailhead.

HORSE CREEK-NORTH FORK TRAIL 🔺 🐎

Length from Horse Creek trailhead to:

North Fork trail junction   5.0 miles, one way.

Cache Creek Trail junction	7.7 miles, one way.
Granite Creek Trail junction	8.7 miles, one way.
Game Creek Trail junction	10.4 miles, one way.
Putt Putt Trail junction	12.0 miles, one way.
Cache Creek parking area	13.7 miles, one way.

Elevation change: Trailhead at 6,211 feet (233-foot gain to Cache Creek parking area, but a 2,189-foot gain to the divide separating North Fork from Cache Creek).

Trailhead: Located up the Horse Creek drainage. This 1.2 mile dirt road begins at Horse Creek Station and ends at a ranch gate that is usually closed.

This trail connects with Cache Creek to make an extensive one way trip through the Gros Ventre Wilderness that either begins at Cache or Horse creek trailheads. For the most part this is a dry trail and relatively unused, except by outfitters and horse packers originating on the Horse Creek road.

The trail begins at the end of the Horse Creek road. A gate to Mill Iron Ranch usually blocks the road. It is possible to park there and venture up the road on foot about two miles where it turns into a trail. The trail fords the stream a few times along the canyon. The trail junctions at the confluence of Horse Creek and North Fork, and the trail continues north through aspen and lodgepole groves to the headwaters of the North Fork. The trail heading east ventures up the headwaters of Horse Creek and eventually connects to Little Granite Creek Trail (see Little Granite Creek Trail for description).

SILVER-HAIRED BAT.

HOARY BAT.

From the upper drainage of the North Fork the trail climbs the divide separating it from Cache Creek. This is the highest elevation and the trail then drops into the headwaters of Cache Creek and follows the Cache Creek Trail (see Cache Creek Trail for description).

LITTLE GRANITE CREEK TRAIL ▲ 🚲 🐎

Length from Little Granite Creek trailhead to:

Head of Little Granite Creek	5.2 miles, one way.
Granite Highline Trail split	6.0 miles, one way.
Highline Trail merge	8.3 miles, one way.
Cache pass	10.8 miles, one way.
Game Creek Trail junction	13.2 miles, one way.
Cache Creek parking area	17.0 miles, one way.

Elevation change: Trailhead at 6,620 feet (176-foot loss to Cache Creek parking area, but a 2,276-foot gain to Cache pass).
Trailhead: The trailhead begins at the end of the 3.1 mile Little Granite Canyon gravel road. The turnoff for this road is located east of Hoback junction on the northside of U.S. highway 187/189. This is a spur road off the Granite Hot Springs road.

This unusual extended hike enters the remote regions of Granite Highline along the base of the Gros Ventre Range. It passes through the Highline region, but starts or ends either in Jackson or the Little Granite Creek trailhead.

The trail is a long extended hike with at least one overnight. Even as a ski tour this trip would require an overnight layover. Because it is in designated wilderness mountain bikes are not allowed. With any mode of transportation a drop off or a car shuttle is needed for this one way trip.

From the trailhead located in a small meadow the trail heads north up Little Granite Creek drainage to its headwaters at the base of the Gros Ventre Range. The first section of trail fords Little Granite Creek several times, usually with log crossings. Several pack trails junction in the upper drainage and it can be confusing to find the correct trail. Keep a keen sense of direction and locate landmarks to traverse this section of trail. After leaving the Little Granite Creek drainage the trail skirts the base of the Gros Ventre Range in a northwest-southeast trending direction. The trail also splits here and re-joins in about 2.3 miles. The upper, or north, trail is easier with less up and down as it follows the contour of the land.

At the base of Cache Peak (10,304 feet) is the pass into upper Cache Creek drainage. From the pass the trail follows Cache Creek Trail (see Cache Creek Trail for description) for 6.2 miles to the mouth of Cache Creek at the parking area.

GRANITE CREEK TRAIL 🔺 🐾

Length from Granite Hot Springs to:

Box Creek	4.4 miles, one way.
Turquoise Lake	11.0 miles, one way.
Flat Creek Trail junction	13.8 miles, one way.
Goodwin Lake Trail junction	13.9 miles, one way.
Granite Highline Trail junction	16.8 miles, one way.
Horse Creek Trail junction	17.5 miles, one way.
Game Creek Trail junction	19.2 miles, one way.
Putt Putt Trail junction	20.8 miles, one way.
Cache Creek parking area	22.5 miles, one way.

Elevation change: Trailhead at 6,987 feet (543-foot loss to Cache Creek parking area, but a 3,153-foot gain to Gros Ventre pass).
Trailhead: The trailhead begins at the end of the 9.2 mile Granite

Canyon gravel road. The turnoff for this road is located east of Hoback junction on the northside of U.S. highway 187/189. At the end of the road is the trailhead and Granite Hot Springs.

This long extended hike into Gros Ventre Wilderness journeys up the remote regions of Granite Creek, crosses the divide and enters Cache Creek to emerge at the town of Jackson. The mid point is Turquoise Lake, a small subalpine lake. The elevation change at the trailheads is relatively minimal by starting at either Jackson or Granite Hot Springs. But either way there is still a 3,100-foot climb through the Gros Ventre Range. By starting at either trailhead provides a great hike with the opportunity for a dip in the geothermal swimming pool.

Granite Hot Springs is located on forest service land and the pool is operated by a concession lease. The developed pool, built of concrete into a hillside, is open throughout the summer and usually during most of the winter. The road, however, for most of the winter is unplowed for about the last few miles, and skiing is required to reach the hot springs from the end of the plowed surface. A fee is required to soak in the springs, even during winter.

The trail is a long extended hike with at least one overnight. Even as a ski tour this trip would require an overnight layover. But it can be done as a long day trip on a mountain bike. With any mode of transportation a drop off or a car shuttle is needed for this one way trip.

From the hot springs developed area the trail heads north up Granite Creek drainage to its headwaters at the base of the Gros Ventre Range at Turquoise Lake. It is primarily a straight trail that follows the drainage north and then veers west at the base of Pyramid Peak (11,107 feet). About 4.4 miles toward Turquoise Lake is a small creek merging from the west. This leads to Box Lake, about 0.7 mile off the trail.

At the base of the Gros Ventre Range is Turquoise Lake, the half way point. From here to the trailhead the trail utilizes the Turquoise Lake Trail and the Cache Creek Trail (see Turquoise Lake Trail and Cache Creek Trail for description) to emerge at the mouth of Cache Creek at the parking area.

SNOW KING MOUNTAIN TRAIL 🚲 ⛷ 🐎

Length: 1.6 miles, one way.
Elevation change: Trailhead at 6,240 feet (1,560-foot gain).
Trailhead: The trailhead begins behind the baseball field on south Cache Street at the base of Snow King Mountain.

The climb up Snow King has been a popular and traditional hike for the residents of Jackson. Most make the hike in the early morning before going to work. And many hikers even clock their ascent, trying to break previous records.

The trail is essentially the maintenance road for ski hill mountain equipment. The trail has a very steep ascent at first, but lessens about half way up into a series of switchbacks. At the summit is a wonderful panoramic view of Jackson and the Teton Range to the distance.

From the summit it is possible to hike or mountain bike other trails, including the backside of the ski hill. One possible route is the Tiny Hagen Trail (see Tiny Hagen Trail for description). This trail traverses east to Cache Creek, ending at the parking area. It is groomed during the winter and also is a good mountain bike or hike during the summer. On the backside there are numerous other trails, tracks, horse trails and roads, including Leeks Canyon. Most hikers, however, return down the same

FROM THE SUMMIT OF SNOW KING, 1950S.

north facing slope of the steepest ski hill for its size in America. But keep a good sense of route finding for whatever path is chosen.

TINY HAGEN TRAIL 🚲 ⛷ 🐎

Length: 1.75 miles, one way.

Elevation change: Trailhead at 7,800 feet (1,356-foot loss).
Trailhead: The trailhead begins behind the baseball field on
south Cache Street at the base of Snow King Mountain.

The Tiny Hagen Trail is a new addition to Jackson Hole's
trail system. The trail is named in honor of Grant "Tiny" Hagen
(1921-1977), an early valley artist who specialized in wildlife
and landscape subjects, portraying them in oil, sketches and
bronze.

This trail traverses Snow King Mountain and begins at the
top of the mountain at the Rafferty chair lift. To reach this point
either the Snow King Mountain Trail (see Snow King Mountain Trail for description) must be climbed or the Snow King
chair lift must be ridden to the top.

From the top the trail traverses the south side of Snow King
east into Cache Creek, ending at Cache Creek parking area.
Prior to 1998 a series of small intertwining trails existed on the
hill side. The trails have been consolidated into a path wide
enough to be groomed during the winter. Thus this provides
an ideal start for cross-country skiers to head into Cache Creek.
For summer activities this trail provides a mountain biking or
hiking trail to or from the mountain summit. The trail, though,
only has a few access points—excluding the Rafferty lift and
Cache Creek parking area—at Cache Creek trailer park, Snow
King Estates and above Snow King Resort.

JACKSON BIKE PATH 🚲

Length: 3.2 miles, one way.
Elevation change: Trailhead at 6,160 feet (no perceptual elevation change).
Trailhead: The bike path begins behind the new post office
between condominium units along Flat Creek.

In the early 1990s fund raising began to construct a bike
path through town to connect outlying residential and developed areas. With donations and matching grants a path was

started by the mid 1990s. The main paved path begins at the new post office on the corner of Powder Horn Lane and Maple Way and follows Flat Creek, past residences and under U.S. highway 189 via a tunnel. It links the high school and middle school and South Park residents. The path cuts through the Brown Ranch and then emerges on highway 22. Once on highway 22 the shoulder of the highway serves as a conduit to the Wilson path, the Aspens (or the Teton Pines path), and Teton Village. Sections of the path are alongside heavy vehicle traffic, but overall it provides a safe passage way.

TRUMPETER SWANS ALONG FLAT CREEK.

Another arm of the path extends south from the U.S. highway 189 tunnel. This paved path connects Rafter J and Melody Ranch. It, in particular, connects Game Creek and provides a safe return for the Game Creek Trail loop (see Cache-Game Creek Trail for description).

Future plans are to extend the path to Horse Creek and eventually Hoback junction via the old highway on the east side of the river.

Other future plans are to extend the paths to include Spring Gulch north into Grand Teton National Park and a better path system through the town of Jackson.

For the most part the path is primarily a summer path, since it is not plowed or skied. During the summer, though, it is heavily utilized by bicyclists and walkers. Some of the path is closed to dogs. But the major drawback is that there are few access points along the path, except at street junctures or if one is fortunate to have the path in their backyard. It is, however, a good alternative mode of safe and a less congested means for walkers and bicyclists to access town and residential areas, avoiding hectic summer traffic.

WOOD'S ROSE.

HIKING TETON PASS & IDAHO

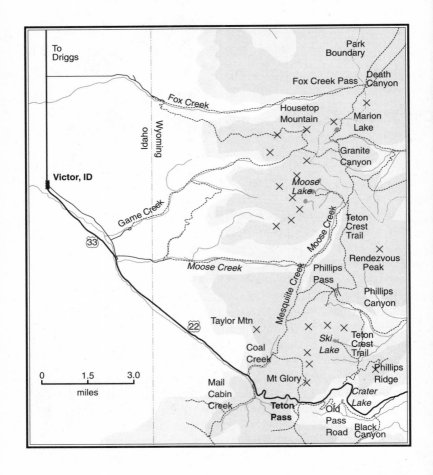

To
Driggs

Park
Boundary

Fox Creek Pass

Death
Canyon

Fox Creek

Housetop
Mountain

Marion
Lake

Idaho

Wyoming

Granite
Canyon

Moose
Lake

Victor, ID

Game Creek

Moose Creek

Teton
Crest
Trail

Moose Creek

Rendezvous
Peak

33

Phillips
Pass

Mesquite Creek

Phillips
Canyon

Taylor Mtn

22

Ski
Lake

Teton
Crest
Trail

Coal
Creek

Phillips
Ridge

0   1.5   3.0

Mail
Cabin
Creek

Mt Glory

Crater
Lake

miles

Teton
Pass

Old
Pass
Road

Black
Canyon

TETON PASS

Teton Pass is known to every local backcountry skier for its easy winter accessibility via the pass road. Because of the 8,431-foot mountain pass and the road that crosses it a whole world of skiing, hiking, horseback riding and mountain biking possibilities suddenly become available.

This region straddles the southern tail end of the Teton Range and the beginning of the Snake River Range, with the pass dividing them. The pass road brings immediate accessibility into the two ranges and their mountain summits and canyons.

CROSSING TETON PASS DURING WINTER.

Teton Pass has a long and prominent history beginning with the Bannock and Shoshone Indians that used this pass on their migrations from lower, warmer wintering grounds to the green, wildlife-filled summer valley of Jackson Hole. By the time fur trappers reached this territory they also used this essential pass to access mountain rendezvous in Pierre's Hole (Idaho) and the rich beaver streams of

Jackson Hole. By then Indian and trapper traffic became so busy that occasional skirmishes broke out on the pass.

The first settlers in the 1880s, primarily Mormon families, moving and settling from Idaho crossed over the pass, using small carts and wagons to transport their meager possessions. After a few pioneers established in the valley the pass became a life link to the rest of the world. Supplies were transported over the pass and, especially, the ever vital mail delivery. To establish a year-round mail route road houses were built at intermediate points along the pass road to provide resting and warming shelters for mail carriers. After a good, but dirt or mud road was established, these road houses were used for other early travellers. By the 1930s car traffic became busy enough that the pass began being plowed. Since then vehicle traffic has exponentially increased, but snowfall and the hazards of keeping the winter road open have not changed.

SAGEBRUSH VOLE.

HOUSETOP MOUNTAIN TRAIL 🐎

Length from Game Creek trailhead to:

Teton Divide	7.2 miles, one way.
Housetop Mountain spur trail	8.2 miles, one way.
Teton Crest Trail	8.1 miles, one way.

Length from top of aerial tramway to:

Middle Fork cutoff trail	3.4 miles, one way.
Game Creek Trail junction	5.1 miles, one way.
Marion Lake spur trail	7.8 miles, one way.

Elevation change: Game Creek trailhead at 6,506 feet (4,031-foot gain to Housetop Mountain) and aerial tramway trailhead at 10,450 feet (an overall 87-foot gain to Housetop Mountain, but first a 1,690-foot loss, then a 1,777-foot gain).

Trailhead: Housetop can be approached from several directions. The primary trailhead is via Game Creek on the Idaho side of the Teton Range, 3.4 miles southeast of Victor on the old road. The other is from the summit of Rendezvous Mountain at the top of the aerial tramway, Teton Village.

Housetop Mountain is one of the mountaineering peaks along the Teton Crest Trail that can be technically climbed or can be hiked along a ridge on the backside. This mountain provides views of Teton Valley—Pierre's Hole—to the west and especially of Borah Peak (12,662 feet), Idaho's highest peak, on the far western horizon. To the east are views of Granite Canyon and the backside of Jackson Hole Ski Resort. It appears the name Housetop was used for several peaks in the surrounding area during the turn of the nineteenth century. By the 1920s the name was finally settled upon for this peak.

The Game Creek route utilizes the Game Creek trail, located northeast of Victor, Idaho. The trailhead is up the canyon about a mile and the trail starts from the parking area. From there the trail follows and makes several crossings of Game Creek to its upper headwaters at Teton Divide.

Just before Teton Divide are several large cirques, and north of the cirques are several peaks, the highest is Housetop Mountain. The trail makes a few switchbacks to climb to the divide and over into Granite Canyon and the Teton Crest Trail (see Teton Crest Trail for description) to connect to the Rendezvous Mountain Trail (see Rendezvous Mountain Trail for description). At the divide follow the ridge line north. A small point (10,214 feet) is climbed first before ascending Housetop Mountain (10,537 feet).

GOOSE WING.

From the summit are great views, including the sheer north face that drops into Fox Creek. Another possible route down is by following the ridge line to the west. It is a faint game trail, but eventually merges with an old two track that made its way up the mountain side. Once this track is discovered it is possible to either junction with the Fox Creek trailhead at the quarry. But the gravel quarry is active and this can be hazardous navigation. The other way is to continue down the old two track to the mouth of Fox Creek. This is a bit longer, but safer and passes by an old Indian and trapper enclosure on Baldy knoll. This route does requires bushwhacking and a sense of direction.

MOOSE CREEK TRAIL

Length from Moose Creek trailhead to:

Footbridge	1.0 miles, one way.
Mesquite Creek trail junction	3.8 miles, one way.
Moose Meadows	4.0 miles, one way.
Moose Lake trail junction	6.5 miles, one way.
Moose Lake spur trail	7.9 miles, one way.
Teton Crest trail junction	6.6 miles, one way.
Moose Creek Divide	7.1 miles, one way.

Elevation change: Trailhead at 6,790 feet (2,275-foot gain).
Trailhead: The turnoff to the Moose Creek road is located 3.5 miles southeast of Victor, Idaho, or 8.5 miles west of Teton Pass on Idaho state highway 33. It is another 2.4 miles to the end of the dirt road and the trailhead at the mouth of Bear Canyon.

This lush canyon trail is a perennial favorite for hikers living on either side of the pass. This trail reaches into the western slope of the Teton Range and accesses the Teton Crest Trail at the boundary of Grand Teton National Park, as well as small subalpine lakes, waterfalls and boggy wildlife meadows.

Moose Creek is a tight, linear canyon that runs west to east with a sharp bend to the north at its upper headwaters. A mile after the trailhead the trail crosses the creek via a footbridge and continues along the north side of the creek.

The canyon is lush with willow, mountain lover, huckleberries, and spirea. The canyon is so lush, in fact, that it is difficult to examine and distinguish the geology of the canyon. For the most part the drainage follows the gently sloping incline of the Teton uplift. The Teton Fault, along the base of the eastern slope, is a fracture zone where the Teton Range rose while the valley of Jackson Hole sank. From the summit of the

Teton Range westward toward Idaho, except for deeply etched stream canyons, it is a relatively smooth, gently sloping landscape.

On the eastern slope of the Tetons the sedimentary layers are gone due to uplifting and to erosion. But on the gentle slope of the westward side the layers remain intact, except for the stream-etched canyons running down its slope. Moose Creek is one of these canyons. Underneath the forested slopes are sedimentary limestones and dolomites. Because of the chemical makeup of these rocks they have a tendency to dissolve in slightly acidic water, such as rain and snow water leaching its way through highly acidic needles and duff on a forest floor. This precipitation as it percolates into the ground follows the natural joints and fractures of the sedimentary rock and gradually, ever so slowly, begins to etch chambers into the weaker layers, creating catacombs and cavities underground.

MOOSE.

To the area north of Moose Creek, all through the west slope of the Tetons, are numerous caves and caverns. Some have exposed entrances and have been discovered, such as Wind and Ice caves. But others have not been exposed and lay dark and hidden under the surface until erosion cuts into a passage.

After about 3.8 miles the trail junctions with the Mesquite Creek Trail (see Coal Creek Trail for description). The trail junction is on the southern edge of Moose Meadows. The meadows, however, is not much of a meadow, rather it is a series of old beaver ponds and a wet marshy area. The trail circumvents most of this, but it can still be wet in early summer. Moose Creek must be forded just above the meadows and this can be treacherous with high runoff.

From Moose Meadows the trail begins a fairly gradual climb until the switchbacks leading to Moose Creek Divide.

Shortly before the switchbacks there are a number of occurrences. One of the most important is a series of two waterfalls, considered the largest on the west side of the Teton Range. They are difficult to see from the trail, and it is possible to walk past them without knowing it. The falls plunge from beside the trail as the trail veers over cliffs above the falls. Two large falls, one above the other, plunge in a notch through the cliffs.

Shortly after the falls the trail junctions twice. The trail continuing up the drainage is a spur trail to a series of small lakes at the headwaters of the canyon. The largest lake is Moose Lake, considered to have a few fish in it. Most of these lakes, however, will be ice covered long into summer. The drainage from Moose Lake disappears into one of the limestone caverns and is very spectacular.

The other trail at Moose Lake trail junction continues up to Moose Creek Divide via a series of switchbacks. After a couple of switchbacks is another trail junction. This time it is the intersection of the Teton Crest Trail (see Phillips Canyon Trail or Teton Crest Trail for description). From this point onward for the half mile to the divide and beyond is the Teton Crest Trail.

At the divide is the boundary of Grand Teton National Park. From here it is possible to connect with the Middle Fork Cutoff Trail and head down the Granite Canyon drainage (see Granite Canyon Trail) or hike to the top of the aerial tramway (see Rendezvous Mountain Trail for description).

COMMON BLUE
BUTTERFLY.

COAL CREEK TRAIL

Length from Coal Creek Trailhead to:

Coal Creek Meadows	1.7 miles, one way.
Taylor Mountain trail junction	2.4 miles, one way.
Taylor Mountain spur trail	3.4 miles, one way.
Coal Creek pass	2.6 miles, one way.
Mesquite Creek drainage	2.8 miles, one way.
Phillips Pass trail junction	3.5 miles, one way.
Phillips Pass spur trail	4.9 miles, one way.

Elevation change: Trailhead at 7,245 feet (1,957-foot gain to Coal Creek pass and a 1,692-foot gain to Phillips Pass).

Trailhead: The Coal Creek trailhead is located 2.7 miles west of Teton Pass on Wyoming state highway 22, or 9.4 miles east of Victor, Idaho. The trailhead at the entrance to the canyon is well marked with a large parking area.

Coal Creek is well-known to Teton Pass skiers who hike up to the summit of Mount Glory to ski the open slopes of the backside and return to the highway via Coal Creek. But the canyon is more than that. It is the southern most canyon of the Teton Range and interconnects with a number of trails on the west side of the Teton Crest. It also is possible from this trailhead to begin the Teton Crest Trail (see Teton Crest Trail for description) and emerge at Cascade Canyon about 32 miles later.

Coal Creek Trail begins at the mouth of the canyon and proceeds up a narrow dark canyon. The trail is somewhat twisted and crosses the trickle of Coal Creek a few times before switchbacking up a slope and entering Coal Creek Meadows. The meadow is not necessarily flat and expansive, but it is more shrubby and open than the lower canyon.

At the northern end of the meadows is the trail junction to Taylor Mountain (10,068 feet). This spur trail crosses over the pass next to Taylor Mountain at nearly 10,000 feet and drops into Taylor Basin. This long arduous trail eventually emerges at the lower canyon of Moose Creek (see Moose Creek Trail for description).

From the Taylor Mountain trail junction it is only a 200-foot climb to the pass (9,197 feet) that separates the heads of Coal and Mesquite creek drainages. Most of the terrain is relatively open, meadow slopes. After the trail drops into Mesquite Creek there is another trail junction. At the Mesquite Creek trail junction the trail either continues following the creek down to its merger with upper Moose Creek after an additional mile, or the trail heads east, upslope to Phillips Pass. The pass con-

MULE'S EAR.

nects to the Teton Crest Trail, or it is possible to go down into Phillips Canyon (see Phillips Canyon Trail for description).

Coal Creek is named, obviously, because of coal veins found along the drainage. These dusty, black veins are occasionally visible in the sedimentary strata. There was an attempt to mine these coal bearing veins, but it was economically unfeasible. To the west, however, in the mountains on the other side of Teton Valley the same veins erupt there. They were mined beginning in 1906 and World War I brought a boom to the mining activity. By 1926 there was even a spur line of the Union Pacific railroad laid to the mines, but afterward the production and the need for coal diminished.

MAIL CABIN CREEK TRAIL 🚵 🚶 🐎

Length from Mail Cabin Creek Trailhead to:

Burbank Creek Trail	1.0 mile, one way.
State line trail junction	3.0 miles, one way.
Mosquito Pass	4.0 miles, one way.

Elevation change: Trailhead at 7,360 feet (938-foot gain).
Trailhead: Mail Cabin Creek trailhead is located 2.4 miles west of Teton Pass, or 8.2 miles west of Wilson, on Wyoming state highway 22. The turnoff is at an acute angle to the road, but it is marked with a small sign. The half mile dirt road leads into the canyon where the trailhead has been used as a staging ground for road construction. A barricade blocks the road at that point.

This dark, narrow, but steep canyon reaches into the northern most section of the Snake River Range. The Snake River Range is separated from the Teton Range, to the north, by Teton Pass.

Mail Cabin Creek Trail heads up the narrow canyon from the trailhead, sited at a construction dump. An old road or a two track leads up the canyon for a partial way, but is blocked off to vehicle traffic at the construction pit.

After the two track ends the trail junctions with the

Burbank Creek Trail which emerges a few miles down the road from the trailhead. From the junction the trail then begins a steep ascent up to Mosquito Pass. The ascent is so steep that for mountain bikers wishing to connect to Mosquito Creek they should walk their bikes either up or down this stretch of trail.

Near Mosquito Pass are a number of old game, horse and pack trails. Most are faint now, but the vestiges of these old trails can be very confusing. Most of the trails head west into Idaho and are long journeys, usually by horseback to their points of origin.

At Mosquito Pass, again, the area is crisscrossed with numerous trails, and it is confusing. Keep a sense of direction and route-finding in mind. From Mosquito Pass it is possible to connect to the Mosquito Creek Trail (see Mosquito Creek Trail for description).

TETON PASS.

This historical route was one of the passages into Jackson Hole and was even noted in Nathaniel Wyeth's July 17, 1832, journal. Later in 1905 Bircher's Roadhouse was built near the mouth of the canyon and provided a rest stop for mail carriers or travelers venturing by horse or wagon over Teton Pass.

TETON PASS RIDGE TRAIL

Length from Teton Pass to:

Mount Glory	0.9 miles, one way.
Black Canyon trail junction	1.5 miles, one way.
Peak 9,236	2.0 miles, one way.

Elevation change: Trailhead at 8,431 feet (1,655-foot gain to Mount Glory or a 795-foot gain to Peak 9,236).
Trailhead: Located at the crest of Teton Pass, 5.8 miles west of Wilson. The two trails start from the pass parking area. The Mount Glory trail heads north and Peak 9,236 heads southwest via a service road.

RED RASPBERRY.

HIKING TETON PASS

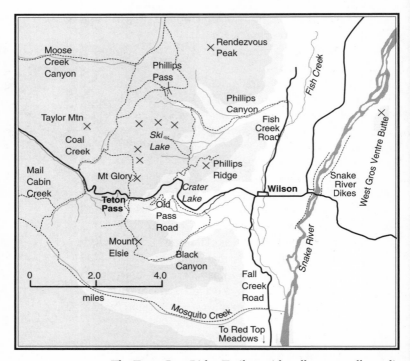

The Teton Pass Ridge Trail provides all-season, all-condition access to the spines of the Teton and Snake River ranges. During mid summer the ridge top trail enters wildflower filled meadows that provide spectacular vistas. During winter the meadows become untracked powder slopes, but still provide spectacular vistas.

The trail heading north from the pass parking area leads directly up the steep embankment. This unofficial trail is the approach to Mount Glory (10,086 feet). The trail is straight up with little or no switchbacks for its 1,655-foot climb. Before and on the summit are a few signs of man. One is a relatively large US West Communications microwave tower that resembles an outdoor theater screen. Another is located just below the summit in the upper bowl of Glory and Twin Slide. These are a series of three propane and oxygen exploders. The purpose of these radio-controlled devices is to send a seismic wave into the ground and create an air blast to trigger an avalanche at its top fault line. This is only done when the road is closed and skiers are off the mountain. A hut on the southside of Glory, by lower Twin, services the exploders with propane and houses the accompanying electronics for detonation.

Still the most commonly used system of triggering avalanches is the use of artillery. The specific equipment has changed over the years, but most are Army Howitzers. There short cannons deliver a high trajectory shell. The shells, however, have changed very little over the years. The shells are 4-inches in diameter, 16-inches long and weigh about 20 pounds. Occasionally they do not explode on impact and these "duds" are found after snow melt. If one of these is found in the area make a note of its location and mark it with a bright color, if possible, and notify either the highway, sheriff or road department. Do not handle or touch these projectiles.

Avalanches have always plagued the Teton Pass road with closures. In 1970 a large arching metal bridge was built across Glory Bowl near the present road. This avalanche bridge was, in theory, designed to allow avalanches to shoot down underneath it. But during construction that first season an avalanche ripped out the bridge and left a mass of crumpled metal frame work at the base near Crater Lake. What remains today is a part of the footings and projecting rebar on the east side of Glory Bowl.

During winter this route up Mount Glory is a popular ski approach. From the pass the trail is mostly a series of kicked-in snow steps up to the summit. At the wind blown summit is a weather station and a large cornice usually forms over the Glory Bowl side. Opposite Glory Bowl, to the west, is a large open powder slope, ideal for telemarking. This slope leads into a coniferous forest, a narrow gully and then converges with the Coal Creek Trail (see Coal Creek Trail for description). The trail then emerges at the mouth of Coal Creek canyon on Wyoming state highway 22, 2.7 miles west of Teton Pass.

To the south of the pass parking area the southern half of the trail follows a service road to a radio tower and high-tension power line. The first mile and a half of this trail also is the beginning of the Black Canyon Trail (see Black Canyon Trail for description).

At the Black Canyon trail junction is a saddle and from there the ridge top trail heads west and continues following the ridgeline of the Snake River Range. The Black Canyon Trail instead heads south and down into the beginning of the canyon. This unofficial ridge top trail from here is faint in some places, but it is possible to explore as much and as far as desired. But keep in mind that this area is a very confusing maze of steep canyons, drainages and ridgelines with no prominent landmarks. Many hikers and skiers have been seriously lost for extended periods in this region. If exploring beyond this area a good sense of route finding and a sense of direction is imperative, as well as appropriate maps, compass, or other location finding aids.

ON THE WAY TO
GLORY PEAK.

The ridge top also is a favorite skiing locale. The trail provides access to some of the best backcountry ski slopes in the region. Numerous open slopes are accessible from the trail and the farther back from the pass the more opportunities there are for pristine untracked slopes. Some of the slopes lead to take out points on the road, including the Old Pass Road (see Old Pass Road for description), but the majority do not. Most slopes lead into a confusing maze of canyons and ravines or to steep walled canyons with treacherous stream fordings. Beware of each ski slope and be prepared to climb back out if the terrain becomes questionable.

BLACK CANYON TRAIL 🚲 ⛷ 🐕

Length: 5.4 miles, one way.
Elevation change: Trailhead at 8,431 feet (1,991-foot loss).
Trailhead: Located at the crest of Teton Pass, 5.8 miles west of Wilson. The trail starts at a service road at the southwest edge of the pass parking area.

Black Canyon is a powerful and rewarding hike along the head of the Snake River Range from Teton Pass. The first section of the trail provides scenic views of Jackson Hole. It then descends into a rather steep, dark, but lush canyon before emerging near Trail Creek Ranch. Even though this is an excellent trail for hiking, mountain biking or skiing it is not as popular as its companion trail, the Old Pass Road, to the north.

The trail begins by utilizing a utility road, skirting antennas and a microwave tower for telephone, television and radio repeater stations. The utility road ends at a high-tension power line tower. This line services the valley from Bonneville Power.

From the high-tension tower the trail narrows and traverses the upper sedimentary cliff-lined catch basin which is the head of Trail Creek. The views from here are spectacular, providing vistas of the Snake River and the pass road, twisting up the mountain side. This is a steep exposure and caution should be taken whether mountain biking, crossing snow patches on foot or traversing on skis. Snow usually lingers on this north-facing slope and in the protection of the trees along the ridge until late June or early July.

The trail wanders along the ridge for about a mile through patches of subalpine fir and Engelmann spruce, and the meadows are dotted with wildflowers even into late summer.

Just before the trail crosses the ridge it parallels a steep cliff and provides the best view. At a pass (9,220 feet) over the ridge the trail leads to the Black Canyon overlook before its steep descent into the drainage of Black Canyon.

The upper head of Black Canyon is dotted with relatively

SILKY PHACELIA.

dense stands of subalpine fir and open, sloped grass and sedge meadows. The trail switchbacks through these.

DANDELION.

Eventually the trail parallels and crisscrosses the small creek of Black Canyon and the last portion of the trail is through a lush and protected forest where the trail is lined by thimbleberry and cowparsnip.

After emerging from the canyon the trail enters a confusing maze of horse trails and old logging roads. It also junctions with the Old Pass Road (see Old Pass Road Trail for description) at the bottom. Take the most used trail that crosses a diversion ditch by means of a log bridge. This trail then joins a dirt road. The exit by this point should head north. The trail emerges onto the paved Trail Creek Ranch road at the "end of county maintenance"—marked as such.

Trail Creek Ranch has had a prestigious owner. Betty Woolsey, America's top woman skier during the 1936 German winter Olympics, fell in love with Jackson Hole and purchased the dude ranch in 1943 and lived there until her death in 1997.

OLD PASS ROAD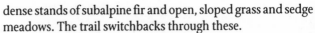

Length from Old Pass Road Trailhead to:
    Crater Lake   1.1 miles, one way.
    Teton Pass   3.7 miles, one way.
Elevation change: Trailhead at 6,603 feet (1,828-foot gain).
Trailhead: Located on the Trail Ranch road. The turn off for this is 1.2 miles west of Wilson on Teton Pass road (WY state highway 22). The trailhead is located at the end of the 1.1 mile paved road where a barricade blocks vehicle traffic.

The Old Pass Road is the all-purpose trail for the Wilson area. This old paved road was once the primary route over Teton Pass before the new realigned highway made this road obsolete. It winds, twists and switchbacks up the mountain side to Teton Pass. Because of its wide and even gradient, although a steep gradient, it is ideal for all activities. Mountain bikes climb or descend the Old Pass Road. During winter it is a popular ski route. Skiers leave cars at the bottom and obtain rides to the pass where they ski down the old road to their parked vehicles. Hikers, too, trudge up the old road and this trail is especially good for hikes with a dog.

The trail begins at the end of the Trail Ranch Road. There a barricade blocks vehicle traffic from continuing up the Old Pass Road. The trail follows the pavement up a moderately steep incline. At about the one mile mark is a small lake, Crater Lake. From there the trail begins a series of switchbacks to the pass. The trail merges with the highway near the summit of the pass.

SKI LAKE TRAIL

Length from Ski Lake Trailhead to:

Phillips Ridge Trail junction	0.4 miles, one way.
Ski Lake Trail junction	1.1 miles, one way.
Ski Lake	2.1 miles, one way.

Elevation change: Trailhead at 7,744 feet (906-foot gain).
Trailhead: Located 4.0 miles west of Wilson on Teton Pass road (WY state highway 22). The highway makes a broad U-turn in the North Fork Trail Creek drainage. Just after the curve, and a half mile before Glory Slide, is a road at a sharp-angle to the highway. On this spur road is limited parking along the edge for a couple hundred feet before a berm blocks vehicle traffic.

Ski Lake is a popular outing for summer or winter, especially as an excursion with dogs. During summer mountain biking or hiking leads through wildflower meadows to a small, circular subalpine lake. In winter there are usually ski tracks leading through forest and meadows to the ice and snow covered lake situated near the Teton Crest.

The trail begins on the old road leading to Phillips Ridge (see Phillips Ridge Trail for description). The road is no longer used and is blocked off with a roadcut berm a few hundred feet from the highway. After about 0.4 mile the trail splits from the old road. Phillips Ridge veers to the east and Ski Lake heads north, but parallels the other trail for about a half mile.

WHITE-FOOTED MOUSE.

Shortly afterward the trail emerges into a clearing and the trail junctions again. This time the trail leading north heads to Phillips Pass and Phillips Canyon (see Phillips Canyon Trail for description), and the trail west continues onward for a mile to Ski Lake. The trail climbs a small ravine, past glacial boulders.

The trail emerges over a rise, through scattered conifers and enters a cirque-like bowl containing Ski Lake. The lake fluctuates. In spring the small lake fills and overflows at its outlet. But as summer progresses and snow and icefields above disappear, the lake level diminishes and the lake becomes shallow with no visible means of an outlet. The outlet stream, however, below the lake usually does have a small trickle. The lake is discharging subterraneanly through the scree slope below the lake and reappearing in the streambed.

SKI LAKE.

The cliffs above that surround the lake are composed of sedimentary rock. Freezing and thawing of these layered rocks have created vast scree slopes of fractured and flattened shards.

PHILLIPS RIDGE TRAIL 🚲 ⛷ 🐎

Length from Ski Lake Trailhead to:
Phillips Ridge Trail junction   0.4 miles, one way.
Phillips Ridge   2.2 miles, one way.
Elevation change: Trailhead at 7,744 feet (698-foot gain).
Trailhead: Located 4.0 miles west of Wilson on Teton Pass road (WY state Highway 22). The highway makes a broad U-turn in the North Fork Trail Creek drainage. Just after the curve, and a half mile before Glory Slide, is a road at a sharp-angle to the highway. On this spur road is limited parking along the edge for a couple hundred feet before a berm blocks vehicle traffic.

Phillips Ridge Trail has the same origins as the Ski Lake Trail, but it is not utilized as much by hikers and skiers.

The trail splits from the Ski Lake Trail after 0.4 mile and continues following an old two track through forest and meadows to the summit of Phillips Ridge (8,442 feet). About a half mile before the summit the trail follows the high-tension power line that crosses Teton Pass to bring power into the valley.

From the ridge is a great view of the valley, especially of the westbank region of the Snake River. At the highest point of the ridge it is possible to continue exploring the ridge to the northeast. The power line, however, does follow the ridge and is highly prominent and visible.

PHILLIPS CANYON TRAIL 🔺 🚴 🎿 🐎

Length from Phillips Canyon Trailhead to:

Phillips Pass Trail junction	3.8 miles, one way.
Phillips Pass spur trail	5.0 miles, one way.
Ski Lake Trail junction	5.5 miles, one way.
Ski Lake trailhead	6.6 miles, one way.

Elevation change: Trailhead at 6,303 feet (1,441-foot gain to Ski Lake Trailhead, but a 1,897-foot gain to Phillips Pass Trail junction and a 2,629-foot gain to Phillips Pass).

Trailhead: Phillips Canyon trailhead is located 3.2 miles north of Wilson on the Fish Creek road. The trailhead is located in dense conifers where the road crosses Phillips Creek. A small parking turnout with a trail heading up the embankment is all that marks the location.

As a quick and easily accessible summer excursion Phillips Canyon Trail is one of the best. This trail reaches into a dark canyon at the southern end of the Teton Range and accesses the Teton Crest Trail at Phillips Pass or small subalpine lakes before connecting with the Teton Pass road.

For a downhill route, especially as a mountain bike trip, this trail can be started from the Ski Lake trailhead. It then ends at the Phillips Canyon trailhead on Fish Creek. This route is a 1,441-foot overall loss, but with a 456-foot gain to Phillips Pass trail junction.

Starting from Phillips Canyon trailhead the trail almost immediately enters Phillips Canyon where the first creek crossing must be forded. There are several fordings, but after spring runoff they are not a problem.

The canyon splits into three forks—North, Middle and South. The trail follows the Middle Fork which is the major fork of the canyon and leads to Phillips Pass. About half way up the Middle Fork the trail junctions. The trail continuing northwest up Phillips Canyon proceeds to Phillips Pass after an additional 1.2 miles. At Phillips Pass the trail connects with either the Teton Crest Trail (see Teton Crest Trail for description) or Mesquite Creek. From Mesquite Creek it is possible to enter Coal Creek drainage (see Coal Creek Trail for description) and emerge at Teton Pass road (WY state highway 22).

At Phillips Pass trail junction the other trail fords the stream and heads south through scattered forests and open hillsides toward Ski Lake Trail junction and Ski Lake trailhead.

This route, especially the downhill direction, is a great mountain bike trip. Most of the trail, except for a few rocky and narrow spots is well suited for mountain bikes. Horse travel also is popular into this area and to the interconnecting trails on the other side of Phillips Pass. This trail, however, in its entirety is not well suited for cross-country skiing. In the upper and middle sections of Phillips Canyon are numerous avalanche paths and their toes dangerously cross portions of the trail.

TETON CREST TRAIL-SOUTH ▲

Length from Ski Lake trailhead to:

Phillips Ridge Trail junction	0.4 miles, one way.
Ski Lake Trail junction	1.1 miles, one way.
Phillips Canyon Trail junction	2.1 miles, one way.
Phillips Pass	3.9 miles, one way.
Moose Creek Divide	8.4 miles, one way.
Middle Fork cutoff trail junction	9.0 miles, one way.
Game Creek Trail junction	10.0 miles, one way.
Granite Canyon Trail junction	10.3 miles, one way.

Marion Lake	11.0 miles, one way.
Fox Creek Pass	12.9 miles, one way.
Mount Meek Pass	16.4 miles, one way.
Basin Lakes (Alaska Basin)	18.4 miles, one way.

Elevation change: Trailhead at 7,744 feet (1,188-foot gain to Phillips Pass, then a drop and another 485-foot gain to Moose Creek Divide, then another drop and a 720-foot gain to Fox Creek Pass and the last 266-foot gain to Mount Meek Pass before dropping into Alaska Basin).

Trailhead: Located 4.0 miles west of Wilson on the Teton Pass road (WY state highway 22). The highway makes a broad U-turn in the North Fork Trail Creek drainage. Just after the curve, and a half mile before Glory Slide, is a road at a sharp-angle to the highway. This spur road has limited parking along the edge for a couple hundred feet before a berm blocks vehicle traffic.

BLACK-BILLED
MAGPIE

The Teton Crest Trail follows the spine of the Teton Range from Teton Pass to Jenny Lake. It is a long extended hike covering 31.4 miles in total length. Most of the trail is a series of ups and downs as the trail drops and climbs into each successive canyon. The trail can be started from either the north end at Jenny Lake or the south end at the Ski Lake Trail on Teton Pass road. The best aspect of the Teton Crest Trail is the numerous canyon trails that intersect it. Side trails provide easy access or exit points anywhere and in any direction along the Crest. So, a trip can be planned for any desired length to incorporate any points of interest. The Teton Crest is essentially composed of numerous segments of other trails and their descriptions can be found in more detail under individual hikes.

RAVEN.

This southern section of Teton Crest Trail covers the trail from Ski Lake on Teton Pass to Alaska Basin. The section from Alaska Basin to Jenny Lake is under Teton Crest Trail-North.

This section of trail uses the Ski Lake, Phillips Pass, Mail Cabin Creek, Rendezvous Peak, Granite Canyon and Death Canyon (see respective trails for description) to Mount Meek Pass and into Alaska Basin.

Hiking Fall Creek-Snake River Canyon

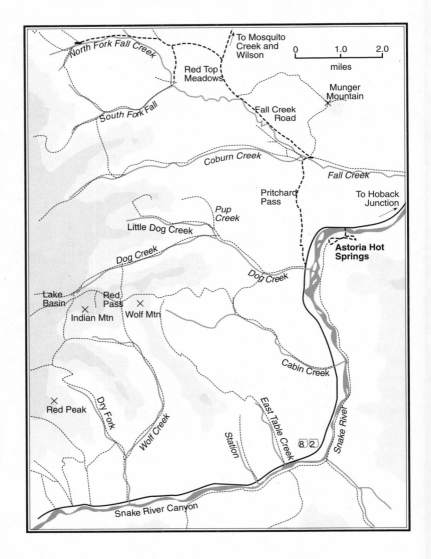

FALL CREEK-SNAKE RIVER CANYON

This extreme southern region of Jackson Hole extends down the Snake River Canyon and includes the Snake River and Wyoming ranges. This region is lower in elevation and thus looses its spring snow earlier, and as a result it is a drier area by mid summer.

The region is marked by the Snake River which winds its way through the mountains and by the two primary roads. One road, U.S. highway 26/89, follows the course of the Snake River. This route is one of the four major entrances into Jackson Hole and usually the only one that remains open during high snow fall years. The other road accessing this region is the Fall Creek/Red Top Meadows road. This gravel road connects Wilson and the Snake River Canyon via low mountain passes and meadows. It also provides access to trails that reach into the remote recesses of this relatively untraveled region.

ELK ON THE ELK WINTERING GROUND.

The trails here are especially great for spring or late fall

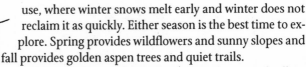

CALLIOPE
HUMMINGBIRD.

use, where winter snows melt early and winter does not reclaim it as quickly. Either season is the best time to explore. Spring provides wildflowers and sunny slopes and fall provides golden aspen trees and quiet trails.

Mountain bike trails in this region wander around rolling hills, down canyons, through meadows, over passes or up steep ravines. While hiking trails ascend peaks that provide panoramic views or meander along mountain streams.

MOSQUITO CREEH TRAIL 🏕 🚲 ⛷ 🏇

Length to Mosquito Pass: 3.6 miles, one way.
Elevation change: Trailhead at 7,000 feet (1,490-foot gain).
Trailhead: The trailhead is located near the end of the Mosquito Creek road. The turnoff for this road is 4.5 miles south of Wilson on the Fall Creek road—at the end of the pavement. After the turnoff it is 5.4 miles of rough gravel and dirt road to a fork in the road and the trailhead.

Mosquito Creek is a beautiful canyon in the midst of Jackson Hole, and in the middle of summer—July—when most hikers are congregated around Jenny Lake this canyon can be relatively uninhabited and peaceful.

Mosquito Creek also provides one of the better and certainly one of the longest mountain bike rides in the region. By extending the route via Burbank or Mail creeks, Teton Pass, Fall Creek and Mosquito Creek roads, the route becomes a very long multiterrain, bike trip loop.

The road up Mosquito Creek is a very rough gravel and dirt road, and in early spring or after a heavy rain the road becomes nearly impassable. The Teton National Forest boundary is about a half mile past the beginning of the road, and camping is permitted in the national forest.

A mile before the end of the 6.4 mile road is a junction. The road leading straight terminates at a dirt berm in about a mile. A trail does originate here—the remnants of an old logging road, but the preferable trail splits at the fork a mile back.

At the road fork the road leading to the north is the true Mosquito Creek trailhead and trail (which may be marked with a misleading outfitter's sign). It is best to leave vehicles at the road fork, since it is a very rough, muddy, rutty Jeep road that also has a treacherous vehicle ford of Mosquito Creek. But this is the only major crossing of Mosquito Creek along the trail, and it is a shallow crossing.

The road terminates after about a mile from the fork at an outfitter's camp. This outfitter's camp, complete with canvas tents and horse corrals, is usually established at the roads end during summer and fall. Unfortunately a hiker must go through camp to continue on the trail beyond.

The trail beyond the end of the Jeep road is a well used trail that follows Mosquito Creek on its north side. The trail, after a short stretch, leaves the heavy lodgepole, spruce and fir forest and emerges into an open meadow of which the creek bottom is lined with a thick covering of willow. The trail skirts the willows at the base of the canyon and wanders along the grassy hillside most of its course to the head of Mosquito Creek.

At the head of Mosquito Creek the trail enters heavy woods again as it makes a few gentle switchbacks up to the pass. Route finding from this location is difficult. It is best to either return to the trailhead or continue on to Coal Creek (see Coal Creek Trail for description) or Burbank Creeks. But numerous game trails and creek drainages emanating from the pass make it difficult to locate the correct trail and direction.

MOSQUITO CREEK.

The other trail, beginning at the end of the Mosquito Creek road that terminates at a berm, was essentially a logging road. Thus it is relatively wide, clear and has moderate gradients, except for occasional berms or runoff trenches created by spring water. Because it was a logging road most of the upper slopes of Mosquito Creek have been logged and large angular clear-cuts mark the southern half of the drainage. During its logging heyday after World War II into the 1970s a sawmill operated at the lower end of the canyon.

After about a mile a tributary of Mosquito Creek was blocked by a mud slide in the spring of 1997. The trail crosses the debris of twisted trees and the jumble of soil and rock.

Toward the head of Mosquito Creek the trail becomes faint and turns into game trails when it enters the forest. There is no official trail here and if one wishes to continue to Mosquito Pass a good sense of route finding and an ability to bushwhack through dense, steep sloped forest is needed.

HAWK MOTH.

NORTH FORK FALL CREEK-COBURN CREEK TRAIL

Length from North Fork Fall Creek trailhead to:

South Fork Fall Creek	2.5 miles, one way.
Coburn Creek	4.6 miles, one way.
Fall Creek road	9.6 miles, one way.
Return loop via Fall Creek road	18.5 miles, loop.

Elevation change: Trailhead at 7,000 feet (721-foot loss, but two small passes at 7,250 and 7,600 feet must be crossed).

Trailhead: The trailhead begins at the end of the North Fork Fall Creek road, just west of Red Top Meadows. This 4.75 mile dirt road junctions with the Fall Creek road at the northern edge of the meadow between several homes and is marked with a county sign. From Red Top Meadows the North Fork Fall Creek road winds and twists up the creek drainage past the turn off to Trail End Ranch and 3 miles beyond that—even though a sign reads 1 mile—is a barricade across the road and a camping area.

The North Fork Fall Creek-Coburn Creek loop is a seldom traveled trail into the Snake River Range. It is primarily a jumping off location for pack trips and outfitters. The North Fork Fall Creek trail is an extended hike, but it is a far better mountain bike trip. In spring clay soils can be unmanageable, but summer and fall are the preferred seasons to use this trail.

The trail begins at the end of the North Fork Fall Creek road. The road ruts continue beyond the barricade and shortly after the trail junctions. The westward heading trail stays on the north side of the creek, but eventually veers north and leads to Elk Creek, a remote region of the Snake River Range.

The North Fork Fall Creek-Coburn Creek Trail continues in a southward heading and crosses the creek and leads up a small tributary. The trail then crosses a low pass after about a mile from the trail junction and drops into a small tributary of South Fork Fall Creek. The trail follows the drainage to South Fork Fall Creek, crosses that stream and continues south up another small tributary to yet another pass.

RUSHES ALONG THE CREEK.

This time the trail drops into Coburn Creek drainage and it is essentially all down hill to the exit at the base of Munger Mountain on the Fall Creek road. However, the trail crisscrosses the stream several times.

Most of the trail from the trailhead to the junction with Coburn Creek is through dense coniferous forest. Once Coburn Creek is reached the forest opens up with meadow slopes, aspen stands and willow bottomland.

The trail emerges at the mouth of the canyon where an old, small plane, landing strip was located. The trail circumvents this and fords the creek to join the road near the confluence of Coburn with Fall Creek at a bridge.

For a return to the trailhead a car shuttle must be made here or a bike ride back to Red Top Meadows and the North Fork Fall Creek road. This return route is 8.9 miles of dirt road.

MUNGER MOUNTAIN TRAIL 🚴 🐕

Length: 2.0 miles, one way.
Elevation change: Trailhead at 6,312 feet (2,071-foot gain).
Trailhead: Located approximately 13.2 miles south of Wilson

on the Wilson-Fall Creek road. A small, blocked turnout marks the trailhead just off the dirt road. The trailhead is unmarked, but it is across from the willow bottom of Fall Creek.

A hike up Munger Mountain, located at the southern edge of Jackson Hole, provides a unique view and aspect of the valley. It is a less traveled trail, but one of the classic Jackson Hole hikes.

There are several approaches to the summit of Munger Mountain (8,383 feet). Most begin at the base of the mountain on the Wilson-Fall Creek road, just south of Red Top Meadows. This section of road parallels the willow bottom of Fall Creek. Several ravines run up the mountain from the road and there are parking areas or short access roads leading into them.

One of the best trailheads is the second ravine after dropping out of Red Top Meadows at the end of the county maintenance. This parking area is characterized by a dirt berm blocking the entrance to the ravine to prevent vehicles from driving into it. From this point the summit of Munger Mountain is due east. There is no designated trail, but it is a simple bushwhack. All that is needed is a good sense of route finding to reach the summit.

LITTLE BROWN BAT.

The old traditional route is located just before the Fall Creek bridge. A spur road heads east off the Wilson-Fall Creek road at a sharp bend in the road, just before the bridge. A quarter of a mile from the bridge is the trailhead. This route was used by the Forest Service to haul supplies to the lookout on the summit during its heyday. This approach from the south is shorter at 1.6 miles, but about the same elevation climb. Either route provides comparable access to the summit.

LONG EARED BAT.

The summit once held a fire lookout, but all that remains today are the concrete corner footings, grounding cables and a few boards. Also on the summit is an exposed outcropping of limestone rock.

This summit, like many mid-elevation mountain summits

throughout the West, attracts mating lady bugs. In mid to late June the cracks in the limestone rock can be packed with masses of orange and red lady bug beetles. During this bug rendezvous they are mating, and thus not eating. Many companies and individuals would collect lady bugs during these gatherings and sell them to gardeners in their fight to control aphids. However, during this time the bugs are not eating and when they are released into a garden they disperse leaving the garden unchanged.

DOG CREEK TRAIL 🚶 🚲 🐴

Length from Dog Creek trailhead to:

Cabin Creek cutoff trail junction	1.1 miles, one way.
Little Dog Creek Trail junction	2.5 miles, one way.
Red Pass	6.0 miles, one way.

Elevation change: Trailhead at 5,842 feet (2,858-foot gain).
Trailhead: Located 1.8 miles south of Astoria Hot Springs, or a half mile south of the entrance to the Fall Creek road. The turnout is an old road running along the base of the foothills among cottonwoods and occasional spruce trees.

Dog Creek is one of the numerous canyons that drain into the Snake River along the canyon south of Hoback Junction. All of the canyons reach into the remote recesses of the lower Snake River Range. Most interconnect within a network or web of trails throughout this region.

The trailhead is located a half mile south of the Fall Creek road junction and elk feeding grounds. It is possible to start from the work camp at the junction, but this approach usually is swamped by springs, ponds and seeps, especially in late spring. The best approach is the old access road from the south. From this approach it is a short and drier hike to the mouth of Dog Creek canyon. An old two track ran into the canyon for about a half mile and from there it is a packers trail into the upper drainages. Numerous cutoff trails connect with parallel drainages, or other trails intersect and junction along the way.

ROUGH WALL
FLOWER.

In spring and early summer the canyon and stream bottom runs with excess water and the hillsides are vibrant green, but the region dries out by late summer. Some streams vanish completely.

CABIN CREEK TRAIL 🏕 🚵 🐎

Length from Cabin Creek trailhead to:

Dog Creek cutoff trail junction	3.7 miles, one way.
Red Pass	7.6 miles, one way.

Elevation change: Trailhead at 5,840 feet (2,860-foot gain).
Trailhead: Located 4.5 miles south of Astoria Hot Springs on U.S. highway 26/89. The turnoff is marked and a short treacherous access road leads to the trailhead.

BRUSHING AGAINST
STINGING NETTLES
WILL GIVE THE SKIN
A STINGING
SENSATION.

Cabin Creek reaches into the deep interior of the southern portion of the Snake River Range. This canyon trail, like others originating from the Snake River canyon, interconnects to a web of backcountry trails via numerous junctions, cutoffs and horse packing trails.

The canyon entrance is very dark, narrow and lush with spruce, Douglas fir and lodgepole trees. The access road off the main highway is a rough dirt two track that should only be attempted with high clearance vehicles. From the trailhead the trail continues up the narrow canyon. It junctions with a cutoff trail to Dog Creek, before heading up to a hydrographic divide dominated by Wolf Mountain (9,483 feet). The trail circumvents the north slope of the mountain before it junctions with Red Pass. At red pass it is possible to connect with Dog or Wolf creeks (see respective trails for descriptions) or to trails leading north.

EAST TABLE CREEK TRAIL 🏕 🚵 🐎

Length from East Table Creek trailhead to:

Wolf Mountain junction	7.1 miles, one way.

Red Pass   7.9 miles, one way.
Elevation change: Trailhead at 5,821 feet (2,877-foot gain).
Trailhead: Located 8.3 miles south of Astoria Hot Springs on
U.S. highway 26/89. The trailhead access road is located across
the highway from East Table Creek campground.

East Table Creek is a great hike for campers staying at the
nearby campground. This Snake River tributary canyon is a
dry canyon beginning among Rocky Mountain junipers and
lodgepole pines.

It is a long hike into the interior of the Snake River Range.
Once into the headwaters and the hydrographic divide near
Wolf Mountain the trail junctions with the Cabin Creek Trail
(see Cabin Creek Trail for description) to connect with a network of different route possibilities.

WOLF CREEK TRAIL

Length from Wolf Creek trailhead to:
   Dry Fork trail junction   1.2 miles, one way.
   Meadows trail junction   5.0 miles, one way.
   Red Pass   6.2 miles, one way.
Elevation change: Trailhead at 5,751 feet (2,949-foot gain).
Trailhead: Located at mouth of Wolf Creek canyon, 12.4 miles
south of Astoria Hot Springs in the Snake River Canyon. It is
not marked, but across the road is the defunct Wolf Creek
campground. Parking is available there or on the alluvial bench
at the mouth of the canyon.

Wolf Creek, like most of the Snake River Canyon hikes,
can be hiked early in the spring season. Mainly because of its
lower elevation and south facing slopes its sheds its winter snow
long before most of Jackson Hole.

Wolf Creek is a narrow, constricted and very shrubby canyon. Alders, chokecherry and red osier dogwoods line the small
creek bottom and rocky, scree slopes cover the steep canyon
walls. For the most part it is an easy trail to follow, since it wan-

KESTREL.

ders along the bottom of the canyon. But there are a number of stream fordings as the trail crisscrosses the streams. There is only one junction in the lower canyon about 1.2 miles from the trailhead. This junction leads up Dry Fork to the base of Red Peak.

The Wolf Creek Trail continues up Wolf Creek to large mountain meadows and a basin at the base of Indian Peak. In the meadows the trail divides again. The north trail leads to Red Pass with Wolf Mountain to the east. This trail makes connections to Dog, Cabin or East Table creeks (see respective trails for description). The west trail circumvents Indian Mountain and follows Wolf Creek to its headwaters. The trail then connects to Lake Basin.

TRAIL REVIEWS

SHORT HIKES (HALF-DAY HIKES)

HIKES	REGION	MILEAGE *	PAGE #
Arizona Lake	Colter Bay	1.2	45
Bar BC Ranch	Moose	1.2	118
Blacktail Butte	Moose-Teton Village	2.3	125
Bradley-Taggart Lakes	Jenny	4.8	113
Brooks Lake	Togwotee Pass	4.4	72
Buffalo Fork	Togwotee Pass	2.9	68
Cascade Canyon	Jenny Lake	4.6	98
Christian Pond	Colter Bay	3.1	55
Coal Creek	Teton Pass	4.9	184
Colter Bay Nature Trail	Colter Bay	1.5	51
Cunningham Cabin	Signal Mountain	0.3	82
Curtis Canyon	Jackson	1.6	163
Ditch Creek	Gros Ventre	5.4	150

HIKES	REGION	MILEAGE *	PAGE #
Elk Refuge Nature Trail	Jackson	2.5	162
Flagg Canyon	Flagg	2.5	30
Goodwin Lake	Jackson	3.0	164
Grand View Point	Colter	2.4	55
Grizzly Lake	Gros Ventre	3.2	155
Hidden Falls & Inspiration Point	Jenny	1.0	95
Jackson Bike Path	Jackson	3.2	176
Lost Lake Trail	Togwotee Pass	1.3	71
Lunch Tree Hill	Colter Bay	0.2	53
Mail Cabin Creek	Teton Pass	4.0	186
Menor-Noble Cabins	Moose-Teton Village	1.0	121
Moose Ponds	Jenny	0.9	94
Mosquito Creek	Fall Creek	3.6	200
Munger Mountain	Fall Creek	2.0	203
Phelps Lake	Moose-Teton Village	3.7	128
Phillips Ridge	Teton Pass	2.2	195
Pilgrim Mountain	Colter Bay	1.8	45
Putt Putt	Jackson	4.5	169
Rosie's Ridge	Togwotee Pass	4.6	69
Sargents Bay	Colter Bay	0.25	48
Sawmill Ponds	Moose-Teton Village	0.7	126
Schwabacker Landing	Moose-Teton Village	0.6	123
Signal Mountain	Signal Mountain	5.0	76

HIKES	REGION	MILEAGE *	PAGE #
Ski Lake	Teton Pass	2.1	193
Snake River Dikes	Moose-Teton Village	2.2	144
Snow King Mountain	Jackson	1.6	175
South Landing	Signal Mountain	0.5	78
Spalding Bay	Signal Mountain	open	82
String & Leigh Lakes	Jenny Lake	3.5	86
Swan Lake & Heron Pond	Colter Bay	2.0	51
Teton Pass Ridge	Teton Pass	2.0	187
Timbered Island	Jenny Lake	2.6	111
Tiny Hagen	Jackson	1.75	175
Waterfalls Canyon	Colter Bay	2.6	49

* Please note: Some mileages are one-way and others comprise a loop.

MEDIUM HIKES (FULL-DAY HIKES)

HIKES	REGION	MILEAGE *	PAGE #
Amphitheater-Surprise	Jenny Lake	4.6	107
Arizona Creek	Colter Bay	7.7	44
Avalanche Canyon	Jenny Lake	5.1	115
Bearpaw Lake	Jenny Lake	5.0	91
Black Canyon	Teton Pass	5.4	191
Blue Miner Lake	Gros Ventre	7.3	156
Cabin Creek	Fall Creek	7.6	206
Cache Creek	Jackson	6.2	168
Clear Creek	Togwotee Pass	9.4	66
Death Canyon	Moose-Teton Village	8.6	130
Dog Creek	Fall Creek	6.0	205
East Table Creek	Fall Creek	7.9	206
Emma Matilda & Two Ocean Lakes	Colter Bay	9.2	57
Flat Creek Ranch	Gros Ventre	5.4	157
Garnet Canyon	Jenny Lake	5.4	109
Granite Canyon	Moose-Teton Village	8.7	136
Hanging Canyon	Jenny Lake	2.4	106
Hermitage Point	Colter Bay	8.8	52
Holmes Cave	Togwotee Pass	4.2	70
Housetop Mountain	Teton Pass	7.8	180
Jenny Lake	Jenny Lake	6.5	92

HIKES	REGION	MILEAGE *	PAGE #
Lake Solitude-North Fork			
Cascade Canyon	Jenny Lake	11.3	100
Moose Creek	Teton Pass	7.1	182
Old Pass Road	Teton Pass	3.7	192
Open Canyon	Moose-Teton Village	10.2	134
Peak 10,552	Moose-Teton Village	6.4	132
Phillips Canyon	Teton Pass	6.6	195
Reclamation Road Trail	Flagg Ranch	4.6	31
Rendezvous Mountain	Moose-Teton Village	13.1	140
Rimrock Lake	Moose-Teton Village	5.2	131
Schoolroom Glacier-South Fork			
Cascade Canyon	Jenny Lake	11.2	101
Shadow Mountain	Gros Ventre	9.8	148
Sheep Mountain	Gros Ventre	3.0	152
Static Peak	Moose-Teton Village	7.4	134
Teton Village Tram	Moose-Teton Village	7.2	138
Turpin Creek	Gros Ventre	4.1	151
Valley Trail-North	Jenny Lake	7.7	109
Valley Trail-South	Moose-Teton Village	7.4	127
Whetstone Creek	Colter Bay	6.4	61
Wolf Creek	Fall Creek	6.2	207

* Please note: Some mileages are one-way and others comprise a loop.

LONG HIKES (OVERNIGHT OR EXTENDED TRIPS)

HIKES	REGION	MILEAGE *	PAGE #
Alaska Basin	Moose-Teton Village	13.9	142
Berry Creek	Flagg Ranch	12.6	33
Cache-Game Creek	Jackson	16.5	170
Enos Lake	Togwotee Pass	10.8	65
Granite Creek	Jackson	22.5	173
Horse Creek-North Fork	Jackson	13.7	171
Huckleberry Mountain	Flagg Ranch	14.5	39
Lava Creek	Togwotee Pass	13.4	64
Little Granite Creek	Jackson	17.0	172
North Fork Fall Creek	Fall Creek	18.5	202
Owl Creek	Flagg Ranch	10.4	36
Pacific Creek	Colter Bay	14.6	59
Paintbrush Canyon	Jenny Lake	22.5	88
Pilgrim Creek	Colter Bay	12.7	47
RKO Road	Signal Mountain	15.5	79
Teton Crest Trail-North	Jenny Lake	13.0	105
Teton Crest Trail-South	Teton Pass	18.4	196
Turquoise lake	Jackson	11.5	166
Two Ocean	Togwotee Pass	12.8	67
Webb Canyon	Flagg Ranch	9.8	38

* Please note: Some mileages are one-way and others comprise a loop.

PHOTOGRAPHIC CREDITS

All other photographs by the author, Carl Schreier, except as
  noted:

page 27) "Bob Kranenberg at the mouth of Cascade Canyon,
  1930s." Photograph by Roland Wolf. Courtesy The Schreier
  Collection.

page 70) "Interior of Holland Chamber, opposite entrance.
  Holmes Cave." Photographer unknown. Courtesy The
  Schreier Collection.

page 77) "The view from Signal Mountain." Photograph by
  W.H. Jackson. Courtesy The Schreier Collection.

page 90) "The Grand from Mount Woodring." Photograph by
  Todd Anderson. Courtesy of the photographer.

page 106) "Aerial of the three Tetons." Photographer unknown.
  Courtesy The Schreier Collection.

page 161) "The View from Snow King Mountain, 1960s." Photographer unknown. Courtesy The Schreier Collection.

page 175) "Winter View from Snow King Mountain." Photographer unknown. Courtesy The Schreier Collection.

page 179) "Victor-Jackson passenger stage, winter, Teton Pass."
  Photographer unknown. Courtesy the Schreier Collection.

BIBLIOGRAPHY

NATURE

Carrighar, Sally. 1947. *One Day at Teton Marsh*. New York: Alfred A. Knopf.

Murie, Maragret and Olaus. 1966. *Wapiti Wilderness*. New York: Alfred A. Knopf.

Perry, William, and editors of Homestead Publishing. 1995. *Rocky Mountain Wildlife of Yellowstone and Grand Teton National Parks*. Moose, Wyoming: Homestead Publishing.

Raynes, Bert. 1995. *Birds of Jackson Hole*. Moose, Wyoming: Homestead Publishing.

Raynes, Bert. 1995. *Wildlife of Yellowstone and Jackson Hole*. Moose, Wyoming: Homestead Publishing.

Schaefer, Vincent J., and John Day. 1981. *A Field Guide to the Atmosphere*. Boston: Houghton Mifflin.

Schreier, Carl. 1996. *A Field Guide to Wildflowers of the Rocky Mountains*. Moose, Wyoming: Homestead Publishing.

Schreier, Carl. 1982 (1996). *Grand Teton Explorers Guide*. Moose, Wyoming: Homestead Publishing.

Schreier, Carl. 1997. *Yellowstone Explorers Guide*. Moose, Wyoming: Homestead Publishing.

GEOLOGY

Schreier, Carl. 1992. (2nd ed) *A Field Guide to Yellowstone's Geysers, Hot Springs and Fumaroles*. Moose, Wyoming: Homestead Publishing.

WILDERNESS

Nash, Roderick. 1973. *Wilderness and the American Mind*. London: Yale University Press.

Editors of Homestead Publishing. 1997. *Yellowstone Hiking Map*. Moose, Wyoming: Homestead Publishing.

Editors of Homestead Publishing. 1998. *Grand Teton Hiking Map*. Moose, Wyoming: Homestead Publishing.

Schreier, Carl. 1997. *Hiking Yellowstone Trails*. Moose, Wyoming: Homestead Publishing.

Schreier, Carl. 1998. *Grand Teton Short Hikes*. Moose, Wyoming: Homestead Publishing.

Schreier, Carl. 1998. *Yellowstone Short Hikes*. Moose, Wyoming: Homestead Publishing.

HISTORY

Bonney, Lorraine. 1995. *Bonney's Guide to Jackson's Hole and Grand Teton National Park*. Moose, Wyoming: Homestead Publishing.

Clary, David A. 1993. *The Place Where Hell Bubbled Up*. Moose, Wyoming: Homestead Publishing.

Sanborn, Margaret. 1993. *The Grand Tetons: The Story of Taming the Western Wilderness*. Moose, Wyoming: Homestead Publishing.

Schreier, Carl. 1989. *Yellowstone Selected Photographs: 1870-1960*. Moose, Wyoming: Homestead Publishing.

INDEX

FOR A COMPLETE LISTING OF OTHER NATURAL-HISTORY
PUBLICATIONS FROM HOMESTEAD PUBLISHING, SEND FOR A
CATALOG. WRITE OR CALL:

Mail order Department
Homestead Publishing
Box 193 • Moose, Wyoming 83012
(307) 733-6248

- -

For reordering please check your favorite bookseller or copy and send this form to:

HOMESTEAD PUBLISHING
Box 193, Moose, Wyoming 83012

Name _____ Phone _____

Address _____

Town _____ State _____ Zip _____

QTY	TITLE	PRICE
	Hiking Yellowstone Trails - retail $14.95	
	Yellowstone Hiking Map - retail $9.95	
	Hiking Grand Teton Trails - retail $14.95	
	Grand Teton Hiking Map - retail $9.95	

For credit card payment—Visa/Mastercard/AmEx

Card number #_____

Expiration date_____

Signature_____

Shipping	$3.00
Please Remit —Total	